*The Magic of Dreams and Spirit Guides*

Also by Robin James
*Messages from Mathias*

# The Magic of Dreams
# and Spirit Guides

## by Robin James

*Shining Hand Press*
*Ashland, Oregon*

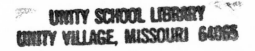

FIRST PRINTING, 1999

Cover Design by David Rupee, Impact Publications, Medford, Oregon
Cover Art by Harriet Rex Smith
Hale-Bopp photograph by Dave Bloomsness
Author photograph back cover by Christopher Briscoe

Printed in Canada


ISBN 0-9675484-0-3

# Table of Contents

# Dedication

This book is dedicated to all the spirit guides and angels who have helped me along the way and will continue to light my path with their love.

It is also for Scott — my husband, my lover, my friend — the angel who has held my hand along the way and who has shown infinite patience and support as I wrote in the mornings, in the evenings, all day long, on airplanes, on vacations, at home, at the office, in every spare moment and in every feasible place.

I especially thank my wonderful mother, Helen, for a lifetime of love, support, and encouragement. It has been a joy and a privilege to be her daughter and her friend.

I also want to thank Al, Diana, Rachel, and Joshua, who have dedicated themselves to bringing the messages of our guides into this dimension.

Many thanks to Mel and Karla who typed my scribblings.

I dedicate this book, finally, to all of my beautiful children — the three here walking the path with me, and the one who is present and yet not in physical form. Thank you for teaching me about love and life and death. Thank you for opening your hearts to the magic.

*Robin*

# Introduction

I have been thinking about writing and sharing my story for a very long time. It is said that everyone has a story to tell. But how to tell it? This morning as the dawn breaks, I am told to allow that Native American part of me to tell it like it is — no embellishment, no flowery prose.

No, I am not Native American, or even part Native American, in this lifetime. But I have lived as an Indian in another place, another time — another lifetime — as most of you reading this have. It is this part of me that writes these words.

This time on Mother Earth is a very special, very exciting time. We are all blessed to be here at this time. We have all chosen to be here. It is easy to forget this in the day-to-day challenges. Most of us have forgotten the magic and the true purpose of our walk here on Mother Earth. Somehow between the ups and downs of life on this Earth at this time, I have been given the gift of glimpsing this magic. It is a gift that is meant to be shared — like all of life's greatest gifts. So come with me now as I walk my walk and talk my talk, and we will remember the magic.

February, 1997

# The Magic of Dreams and Spirit Guides

Chapter 1

# The Psychic Connection

*We are all angels, "For that is the source of origin of all souls. Many define angels as those souls who have never left God's side, and no one ever leaves God's side."*
*~ Lama Sing*

*I* am sitting on the kitchen floor as a very young girl, perhaps three or four years old, and the family Siamese cat, King, is sitting next to me. We are very comfortable with each other, for we know each other well. King and I talk to each other regularly, telepathically.

This memory returns to me recently as I am seated with a group of people experiencing a past life regression. I have few childhood memories. If you were to ask me if I had a happy childhood, I would say "yes." I had wonderful parents and a very loving family and all the comforts and advantages of being raised in upper middle class America. But why do I have such little recollection of my childhood, and why have I always felt so alone?

Merlin, the Madcap Magician from Mars, tells me it is because as a child, I believed in and practiced magic. But no one around me supported, encouraged, or participated in my wizardry. Being a newly entered angel and seeing with much more than earthly sight, I was often confused by the mixed messages I received. What I observed in the Earth was many times disappointing to my knowledge of the light. The people around me, children and adults alike, often felt uncomfortable in my presence when I spoke my truth. I quickly learned that what I perceived and knew in my heart to be truth was many times not perceived or accepted as such in the world around me.

So I shut down many of my abilities with which I had entered into Mother Earth, as a protection and in an attempt to conform to the belief system around me. For how could I exist in a world that was full of such discrepancies with the truth and the light? For many, many years, I operated with only half of my true awareness; for that was the only comfortable way for me to function in the Earth at that time. I continued, however, to see much more than those around me with my spiritual eyes, which created quite a bit of pain and confusion for me at times. I could always see the truth behind others' actions, no matter how contrary to their words. So the magic faded from my life, not to be reawakened until many years later.

# The Psychic Connection

I married at age 23, had two children and was living with my family in a large house with several other people in Tallahassee, Florida. My interest in magic was reawakened when I was told about Edgar Cayce, the sleeping prophet. I was fascinated with his life and work and read everything I could find about him. I tried many remedies recommended in his readings and found them incredibly helpful for myself and the children. Other books I read that were popular at the time were those written by Jane Roberts, Ruth Montgomery, and Carlos Castaneda. All of these people helped me to realize that magic was alive and well on Mother Earth.

One of our housemates told me that he had a personal friend, Al, who did channeled psychic readings like Edgar Cayce had. Al's ability to enter into a sleep-like state of hypnosis, from which readings might be obtained, was discovered by accident as a result of a "chance" hypnosis session. At the time, he had no conscious knowledge of metaphysical topics. In fact, he had worked in the field of computers for 13 years. Lama Sing is the name of the collective group of souls that speak through Al when he is in trance. I learned that Lama Sing rarely made predictions about future events and never gave information that would interfere with one's free will.

My friend had recently had a reading with Lama Sing and offered to share it with me. Al does the reading without the subject present, tapes it, and then sends the tape. What I heard was extremely loving, supportive, and spoke to my heart as the highest truth. I immediately sent in my $26 donation along with several questions.

This began an association which still continues to this day, some 20 years later. I consider Lama Sing one of my spirit guides, a counselor who has enlightened my path immeasurably, enabling me to view my life experiences and relationships from a timeless, spiritual perspective which has changed my life and allowed me to grow in wisdom and in love. He always encourages one not to become dependent upon his guidance, but rather to go within for the highest guidance of all. But for those times when the waters of life become muddy and our vision is unclear, guidance from Lama Sing as well as others is available.

Lama Sing, like Edgar Cayce, is able to assess the physical body for imbalance or disease and recommend the very best treatment specifically for the subject's body, as well as address the root of the problem at the mental, emotional, and spiritual levels. He has taught me that illness on the physical level is usually the manifestation of a lack of ease, or dis-ease on the other levels, or something the soul has chosen to fulfill a karmic debt or opportunity.

Lama Sing and some of the other psychics I've worked with are also able to access past life experiences that may be responsible for, or contribute to, a challenge in the present. Counselors or psychiatrists may take weeks, months, or never uncover the source of an emotional problem, and sometimes one can spend much time and money at doctors' offices without getting help. The answers I've received from readings have proven to be highly accurate and have addressed my concerns from a truly holistic perspective.

# The Psychic Connection

We are never alone. Each of us has guides and angels whose purpose and privilege it is to love us, support us, encourage us, teach us, and guide us in any way that does not interfere with our free will or universal law. Some of these companions in spirit have been with us since the beginning of creation and will continue to guide us throughout eternity. Others join us on our paths much like our school teachers on Mother Earth, assisting us and imparting their knowledge to us until we have graduated to the next level and another teacher. Our guides learn and benefit from their experiences with us, just as we do, as a result of our connection with them. One who does not believe in guides and angels is nonetheless assisted in this way. Those who are aware of this relationship and communicate with their spirit guides benefit even more, as the pathway between their dimension and ours is more easily traveled when there is acknowledgment of this relationship. The information, the guidance, and the love are accessed much more easily when one requests this help and is open to receiving it.

Our guides speak to us in many ways — in dreams, during our meditations, in thoughts that seem to just "pop" into our heads. As is the case with Lama Sing, they can speak directly to us, answering very specific questions through those who offer themselves as psychics or channels, as Al does.

In my first reading, I asked for guidance on how to deal with my 18-month-old daughter who was very difficult, throwing temper tantrums constantly. I was shocked when Lama Sing told me that her behavior was a blessing to me, teaching me in many ways, and that she and I had been together in many other lifetimes as the closest of companions. This was a perspective I had never imagined, and the first time I remember being encouraged to step outside the emotional context of events in my life to see the higher purpose of the drama. The information that I received in that first reading, and all successive readings since, was given in an extremely empowering way and resonated within my heart as truth.

In 1986 the Voyager Group was formed. It consisted of a group of individuals who paid to receive readings by Lama Sing on specific subjects known as Voyager Projects. We received both the tapes and the transcripts through the mail and then could submit questions about any of the information which were then answered in "Question and Answer Readings." These Voyager Projects continue to this day and have included subjects such as prayer, universal law, healing with crystals, and dreams. For the last several years, the readings have followed a man named Peter as he left the Earth plane, met his guides who assisted him through the transition, and continued his journey on the other side. Because of the readings, I began praying, meditating, recording dreams, and keeping a journal.

There was a man now known as Joshua who also channeled information from my spirit guides for a number of years when Al was concentrating his energies on the Voyager Projects and was not doing personal readings. Once when I asked through Joshua the reason for a recurrent gum infection, I was told that I was being critical of myself or someone else. I knew immediately what he was referring to; I stopped criticizing someone close to me, and the infection disappeared. Another time Joshua told me that the reason for stomach trouble I had been bothered by for months was that I was allowing unfairness in my life. My ex-husband, in his anger, was refusing to pay child support. Not wanting to go through the hassle of going to court, I had decided not to pursue the matter. However, as my spirit was telling me through my body, it was simply not fair. I began legal proceedings and had no more of the stomach trouble.

Now I try to pinpoint, on my own, the dis-ease on the mental, emotional, or spiritual level that is responsible for each physical ailment. Last year I had what I described as a "stabbing" pain in my upper back for several weeks. Nothing I did on the physical level helped. I finally realized, through my own description of the pain, that emotionally I felt I was being stabbed in the back by someone. My teenage daughter had lied to me, quit school and generally had made my life a living hell. I had gone through similar experiences with her brother and sister, and intellectually, I knew that this was just a part of her growth and her fight for independence. I didn't realize until the physical discomfort, however, that emotionally I felt as though she were stabbing me in the back. After discussing my feelings with her honestly, the pain disappeared.

My companions in spirit have always encouraged me to seek the medical help that is available from the "white-coated gentlemen" when needed. Once I was

7

told by Lama Sing that I had an infection that I was totally unaware of and that I should go to my doctor to get the appropriate antibiotic, for my system was in a weakened state and was unable to fight the infection effectively without the help of an antibiotic. An infection was subsequently discovered and treated by my doctor!

Lama Sing and the other angels who have spoken to me through channeled readings have given me impeccable guidance and tremendous love and hope along my path. My spirit has been buoyed by them during times of great adversity and challenge. During the past 20 years with their help, and through my desire and determination to serve the light and our Creator, the veils have been lifting. One by one — slowly and extremely painfully at times — my perceptions of reality have become clearer. In the process, the magic once again lives, in my heart and through my experiences.

## Chapter 2
# *Birth*

*Meet adversity with a smile, and if need be, laughter;*
*and it will empower you not only to endure,*
*but to ascend above any challenge.*
*~ Lama Sing*

*I*n 1979 I was licensed as a massage therapist. I loved helping others and being self-employed. I soon discovered, however, that after working with some people, I seemed to have taken on their physical ailments. Obviously, a lot more than just working with muscles was occurring during my work. Once again, I wrote to Lama Sing. He recommended that upon conclusion of each treatment, I dispense the energies from myself and from the patient unto the God center, and that I cleanse and then close myself after completing the treatment so that there would not be the carry-over of energies or forces which could be latent in and about me from one subject to the other. This might be as simple as wearing an outer cloak that could be changed several times, or to spiritually, mentally, and physically cleanse the hands or the body's auric field. Usually a very pastel blue or green will reflect these energies and not absorb them, whereas yellows, whites, browns, and beige tend to absorb and hold such energies. It was also suggested that I wear some topaz or turquoise, as these stones tend to provide a balance and emanate an energy which balances the auric energy.

Lama Sing told me that I had been involved in similar work in previous lifetimes: "In the Atlantean, working to relieve those entities of the thought forms they had constructed for themselves. In the Persian, involved in the aspects of healing. In the South American, as a part of a ceremony which was used for purification. In the English, as a part of a quasi-religious medical activity. In the North American, further as a part of normal knowledge for healing using herbs, potents, massage, magnetism, and other forces known to the natives of the North American in times past."

I learned that massage is often much more effective if one soaks for 20-25 minutes in a warm Epsom salts solution. This makes the body more receptive and tends to dissipate subcutaneous blocks or energy imbalances. Whenever possible, soaking within one to two hours before the massage is the most beneficial. These baths have been a tremendous help to me personally in times of physical imbalance and mental and emotional stress.

## Birth

An important part of the process of healing is simply taking the time and trouble to take care of self.

Lama Sing said that not only the energy released during my work was affecting me, but also the energy of Mother Earth. As geographical disruptions occurred, they affected me subliminally when I opened myself to serve as a channel of healing energy. At times I would feel strange energy shifts within my body and discover that a major earthquake or volcanic eruption had occurred somewhere on the Earth. Obviously, we are affected by much more than we know. We are deeply connected to the Earth.

Soon after this reading, I learned that I was pregnant with my third child. Working throughout the pregnancy, I was not aware of taking on energy from my clients. When my water broke, my pains never began, and labor had to be induced. A beautiful baby girl was born. I nursed her as I had my other two children. There were problems that never occurred with the others, however. One of my breasts kept getting infected. Then the baby began having some rectal bleeding. Believing that she was allergic to something I was eating, I left certain foods out of my diet, but the bleeding continued. My doctor had no answers. I was frantic.

Lama Sing was consulted, and I was told that my daughter was allergic to my milk and should be raised on raw goat milk. Since I loved nursing, I was devastated but immediately followed his advice. Not only did the bleeding stop immediately, a nasty rash also disappeared. Lama Sing did not explain why she was allergic to my milk, but I soon knew.

I became very ill and was bedridden. Unable to sleep, I was totally exhausted. I had very strange sensations up and down my legs, or my legs would have no feeling at all and feel like lead. I seemed to have no control over my thoughts. Paranoid thoughts raced through my head, and I feared that either I was having a nervous breakdown or was going crazy. My doctor did no tests, but asked me if I had somewhere I could go to rest. I took the baby with me to stay with my parents for a couple of weeks while my husband and other children remained at home. My symptoms did not improve. Life was hell.

Sending off for another emergency reading with Al, I prayed that I would make it through each day. Not knowing the cause of an illness is perhaps the most difficult thing to deal with. Lama Sing informed me that I had a magnesium deficiency as well as numerous glandular imbalances. He explained that during pregnancy a woman is exceptionally receptive. While giving massages throughout my pregnancy, I had taken on errant energy that was released from my patients. One's electromagnetic energy is controlled by the glands, thus all of this errant energy resulted in my glandular imbalances. My first thought was that if working as a massage therapist could be so imbalancing, I never wanted to work in that capacity again. Of course, just after this thought, as I listened to the tape, Lama Sing emphasized the importance of continuing my work and learning to control the energy.

I was given a very specific diet consisting mainly of fish, whole grains, cooked greens, and goat milk. I drank water that had been put in the sun for several hours in a jar surrounded by either green or yellow transparent plastic. Epsom salts baths several times a week were to be followed by massages given in a certain way. Advised to walk daily, I could only go a short distance to begin with, I was so ill. Following Lama Sing's instructions to the letter, I slowly began to improve. It was a full year before I felt well and courageous enough to return to work. I felt I had been through hell and back, but I recovered completely. One of the main things that gave me hope and courage to go on during that year were Lama Sing's words: "You will endure throughout this experience and others, and you will emerge radiant, full of light, and with love."

## Chapter 3

## *Death*

*M*y father was the third child in his family and was born under the astrological sign of Leo. I was the third child in my family and was a Leo, and my third child was also born a Leo. She was born at 8:20 p.m. on 8/20/80, and my father's date of birth was 8/ 2/20. I believe that there is a close spiritual connection between my daughter and her grandfather. However, they were not to know each other for long on the Earth.

One morning in the spring of 1983, I went to visit a good friend. She told me that she had seen my father in a dream the night before, and he had asked her to take good care of me. Later that afternoon, I received a call telling me he had died that morning. Sudden death is such a blessing for the one leaving, but so painful for those left behind. My parents had a wonderful marriage, an example to all those who knew them of a healthy, joyful, and fulfilling relationship. So of course, my mother, a most loving and dedicated wife, experienced the most pain as a result of my father's sudden departure.

I loved my father deeply. We were very close. He was a very special and wonderful man who was loved by everyone who was lucky enough to know him, a person who left a trail of love and light wherever he went. He taught me to see and acknowledge the good in each person and encourage it.

In a recent Voyager Project, Lama Sing had these words concerning death:

"How can a death be a blessing? Well, difficult to speak on this in generalities, but often we see that souls who remain in the Earth after loved ones have crossed over through the veil learn a great deal about themselves and their relationship with the entity who has departed, and so on and so forth. There is the search for meaning in life and within self. There is the quest for understanding of what lies ahead. All of these, and much more, transpire on the part of those who remain behind. And the effect is profound. So, none can, in truth, from a spiritual vantage point, dispute the potential that is found in such an event.

"This lessens very little the sense of loss. This we know. There is a sense of loss here, in these realms, that is similar to what you experience when a dearly loved companion leaves these realms to incarnate in the Earth. Think of that for a moment or two. Certainly, the one who loves this newly incarnated entity can visit, can walk with that entity; but it's not the same, is it? No different than it is for you when you think about a loved one who has gone beyond the Earth. You can look at photographs, perhaps listen to recordings or television recordings, and touch clothing and all that sort, perhaps even interact with them in the dream state. But something (is missing) — that capacity to reach out and touch, to hold them and their energy close to your own, the loving embrace, the opportunity to look into their eyes, to hear and feel who and what they are.

"But if you look at this from arm's-length, so to say, for a moment, think about what wondrous gifts you have received and given. And think about the fact that you are still capable of giving these to others in the Earth. And think of the meaning, think of the blessing that this could be to someone else. Think of the honor, the contribution of an affirmation of sorts, which is testimony to the love you have shared with one who has gone on. To close down, to limit self, to place a shell around yourself and keep it all within — those are un-opened gifts. Those are blessings unbestowed. See?

"It is good for all of you to look around you at those who are with you in your family, and to hold the thought of them for a moment in comparison to life without them. See? Each moment is precious. It is an opportunity to create. What you create when you do so with a loving attitude is most profound and is an eternal gift.

"When you proceed through a process of transition which is lengthy in nature, you are afforded some gradient factor of release, of course. Some cannot find this to be true; but the reverse is true that they intensify their feeling of loss, and they intensify their sorrow and, thus, they tend to hold onto the one who is trying to depart. So both are potentials here and have validity of exploration within self. The significance, as we perceive it, is that in the long transitional process there is a gentle time afforded those who will remain behind to explore, to discover, and to realize — wherever there is evidence of such — that certain feelings, certain thoughts, words, or deeds have not been to that point expressed to fruition, to completeness. And so, they are afforded a certain grace, both in time and in spirit, to complete these things and to, in colloquial terms, feel good about the entire event and, ultimately, about having released their loved one.

"In the abrupt transition, as an accident or such, this can still be accomplished.... In essence, no thing is without its potential gift and/or blessing to all involved.

Perhaps a key, then, is to look for that, that this can be sort of healing balm to the wrenching feeling of loss that is accompanying a sudden transition. See?

"The willingness or lack of same for individuals to release a loved one seems to be, as we perceive it, no greater or lesser by culture or by religious belief and/or doctrine — even though outwardly some would seem to have greater ease in this regard. We have looked upon many entities who believe in the continuity of life and have seen their inner grief at a great level of magnitude, and also seen that they had no way to release it because their belief structure afforded none, in the literal sense. They may have been taught from early childhood that life is eternal, given repetitive, demonstrative opportunities to see this, to learn it, to know it. And still, the grief, the sense of loss, cannot utterly be mitigated by a religious doctrine. It is balanced with, inside of self, dependent upon what we would call the completeness of the relationship at the point of transition. Again, this seems to clearly support the importance of living in a state of joy and living with an attitude that frees you to express your love for others. And equally important, to receive love from others, as well, as same is directed to you."

Some months after Dad's death, I was sitting on my porch alone. I saw a beautiful blue light. As soon as my mind went to work attempting to figure out what the light was, it disappeared. I was left with a feeling of peace, of wonder, and of familiarity. Blue was my father's favorite color, and I felt that perhaps he had paid me a visit. Soon afterwards I asked Lama Sing how Dad was doing on the other side, not mentioning this experience to him. He told me a bit about him, and then he told me that I would know his presence by the beautiful blue light, still his favorite color.

*Death is not extinguishing the light.*
*It is putting out the lamp because the dawn has come.*
*~ Unknown*

Chapter 4

## Guiding Dreams

*D*reams are oftentimes simply the expression of emotions we experience in our daily lives, but there are also many other types of dreams. Soon after Dad died, I began having what I call guiding dreams.

The first one I remember was one night after I had decided to call my chiropractor for a neck problem. In my dream I saw a woman's face surrounded by a beautiful white light, and my neck pain was healed. When I woke up, I realized that I knew the woman. She had come in for a massage after one of my patients had given her a gift certificate. I knew she was a chiropractor, but had never considered using her services myself. I deduced from my dream that I should make an appointment with her, which I did. When I told her about my dream, she told me that one other patient had dreamed that she should see her. Laughing, I told her that I thought her getting into other people's dreams was an effective and inexpensive way to advertise. As in the dream, I was healed, and she treated me and my family for years. Her treatments were always effective.

Another time, I dreamed that drinking beer made me sick to my stomach. Soon after that dream, drinking a beer did upset my stomach, and I gave it up. Many of my dreams give me guidance as to which foods I should or shouldn't eat. In one, I was told not to mix fruit or fruit juice with goat milk. In another, I was told I was eating too much fish. Sometimes in a dream, I am eating a plate with certain foods on it, and I know this is guidance as to which foods are beneficial for me at that time.

When I was planning a trip to Bali, I dreamed that I had typhoid fever. It was a torturous dream — I really experienced the pain and agony of that illness while in the dream state. After awakening, I looked up the symptoms of typhoid fever, and this revealed the truth of my dream. Until that dream, I had not planned on any inoculations for the trip. That certainly changed my plans!

Dreams have oftentimes been about my children, helping me to understand something they are experiencing that I might otherwise not realize. When my younger daughter was about ten years old, I had several dreams that she had died. I intuitively realized that these dreams represented the death of the little girl and not an actual physical departure from Mother Earth. Soon after these dreams, my daughter began experiencing some rather intense ups and downs emotionally which I recognized, as a result of the dreams, as the beginning of puberty.

The connection between the firstborn child and a mother is extremely strong. I have had many significant dreams about my son. When he was about fourteen years old, I dreamed that he called me on the phone, and in a very weak and pleading voice said, "Mom, save me."

I literally sat up, waking myself up, yelling, "Save you from what?" When I related the dream to him and asked what I needed to save him from, he had a look of fear in his eyes, but denied knowing the meaning of the message. Soon afterwards I found a roach clip in the laundry used for smoking marijuana and thus became aware of a drug problem. His spirit was obviously asking for my help.

One year when I was on a trip in Barbados, I woke up feeling that my son had been injured in some way, but that the injury was not serious. Calling to check on this, I was told that all was well. However, within a week of my return, he was involved in an altercation at a dance and required stitches in his face.

Recently I had the following dream: *My son is talked into parasailing with a man who is going to take him but really is not experienced enough to know what he is doing. There is an accident, and my son lands on the beach, alive, but badly injured with many broken bones.*

I called my son and told him of my dream. A week

later he declined a friend's invitation to go hang-gliding.

Many years ago, before I was even aware of exactly what echinacea is and what it's used for, I dreamed that one of my massage patients was in need of this herb.

Not only can dreams be the means by which we receive important guidance or prophetic information, they can be memories of past lives, or they can be events that actually occur during that time when our spirits leave our physical bodies and have experiences in the non-physical realms. A good friend of mine who occasionally came for a massage with me told me that one night she dreamed that I worked on a back problem that had been troubling her. When she woke up, her back was totally healed. I told her I was happy to be able to save her the time and expense in the physical world by my visit to her during our sleep states.

I ask for and receive much of my guidance during the dream state. God and our own Higher Selves can speak to us clearly at these times. Our spirit guides encourage us to ask for their help before we go to sleep, which enables them to speak to us in this manner. One only has to believe this is possible to further open and expand the lines of communication. Then it is important to have faith that what we receive is truly guidance.

Chapter 5

# The Harmonic Convergence

*I* had many life-changing experiences during the summer of 1987 when I was 37 years old. During one of my meditations, I heard a loud, clear voice say the word "yoga." I assumed that the message was that I was to begin taking a yoga class, which I did. Practicing yoga that summer was, as it still is in the present, invaluable in assisting me to maintain a sense of balance on all levels.

I needed all the help I could get that summer, for I began to have periods when I would cry for no apparent reason. I did not feel depressed, and these periods seemed totally unrelated to anything going on in my life at the time. Waves of sadness just seemed to pass through me. I would cry and then feel a sense of relief and unburdening. I felt as though I was experiencing a cleansing that was unrelated to the present — that past emotions were somehow being pulled out of me.

Around the same time, I was encouraged by a massage therapist to do a liver cleansing by taking some very mild Chinese herbs. I made the mistake of having a couple of alcoholic drinks at a party about a week after beginning the treatment, and I began feeling quite ill and imbalanced. I had a burning sensation in my stomach and felt a lot of pressure in the front of my throat in my thyroid gland.

I consulted Joshua and was told that I was not alone in the physical and emotional discomforts I was experiencing. Those in the Earth who were seeking to be "channels of blessings," or to bring forth the manifestation of the Christ consciousness into our realms, were undergoing all sorts of activities intended to increase the levels of energies along the pathway from the Earth plane to other realms. The glandular or endocrine centers were the bridge between the two. I was told that the energies of those centers were being balanced and intensified, and that the discomforts that I and others were experiencing were the by-product of the processes of the intensification and purification processes in which drosses were being removed from the physical, mental, and emotional levels within each soul seeking to be within this consciousness.

Astrologically, according to my guides, there were several planets in retrograde which were assisting through heightening the energies and pulling forth the more subtle drosses which were not clearly apparent at the level of the conscious mind but were clouding or limiting me and others.

Added to this general theme of what was occurring, the Chinese herbs combined with the heavier drosses of the alcohol had caused a fermentation of sorts within my body which had resulted in the production of chemicals similar to an internal carbon monoxide. Difficult to eliminate, these chemicals were stored in my liver and several glands.

Furthermore, Joshua said that the sensation in my thyroid was my own soul calling to me, in a sense, to address activities in my life which were no longer productive or useful in my spiritual growth and progression.

It was suggested that I drink lots of water, eat or eliminate certain foods, and take saunas and Epsom salts baths several times a week. Certain yoga techniques as well as meditation were recommended. I was to eliminate dairy products for a while because "there's a coating around each molecule which has the potential of attaching itself to the drosses which are in the body and thus preventing the more rapid elimination of the toxins." I appreciated this explanation, for Lama Sing oftentimes suggests eliminating dairy products when one is trying to cleanse or heal an illness.

I asked the purpose of my illness, and Joshua answered: "Well, the purpose of the illness — and this could be stated as a general commentary on the purposes of many illnesses — the primary purpose of illness is to slow you down, to bring the body, if need be, to a halt, or to a decrease in activity that you might first of all assess that in some way your actions, your behaviors, have not been contributive to the maintenance, to the well being of the vehicle by which you perform your work in the Earth.

"And through the inactivity, to give you a period of time to look at your intent, the actions, behaviors of your life in general, the relationships in your life that are unproductive in the sense that they do not contribute to your joy, your peace of mind.

"And to determine how and if you wish to continue with these, what changes or alterations you need to make, and essentially, is the pathway you are taking under the intent, the surest and quickest method of reaching that goal, that destination?"

The illness was intended to slow me down — a benevolent act on the part of the universe — to give me a period of time to reassess my life that perhaps I might not otherwise have taken.

I was told: "The Earth is entering into a critical time, and all of you who are within that consciousness known as the Christ are being asked to arm yourselves in the most perfect, most aligned armors so that when you enter into the vineyards in order to do your works, you might be properly prepared to perform whatever task your Father has laid before thee."

I was encouraged to begin to place my own needs, values, and desires on a level equal to everyone else's. According to Joshua, "This one activity alone is likely to accelerate your growth to such a degree that you could be moved beyond the potential necessity of one to two incarnations following this current one."

Not feeling well enough to work, I was told I should be able to return to work in a couple of weeks. That would have been about the beginning of August. By that time I had greatly improved and was looking forward to getting back to work. However, then I began to feel very strange — not ill as I had been, but perhaps imbalanced in some other way. I didn't know what was happening to me. I read about something called the Harmonic Convergence in the comics. Doonesbury referred to it as "the Moronic Convergence." I learned that it was some kind of planetary alignment that was to occur around my birthday, August 18th.

On August 16th, my husband and I were out to dinner with friends. I began to feel an incredibly powerful energy coursing through my body. I held onto the arms of my chair and told my husband and friends what I intuitively felt — that I was actually experiencing the energy of the Harmonic Convergence, whatever that was. Or was I just crazy? I'm sure we all wondered if that wasn't really the case!

For the next few days as this intense energy continued to rush through my body, I was only able to sleep a few hours a night. Not in the least bit tired, but amazingly energized, I felt I could barely feel what was actually going on in my own body, the energy was so overpowering. All of my senses were heightened, and everything I looked at seemed to be pulsing with energy. Colors were very intense and vibrant. I was thankful for the "magic" mushroom trips I had experienced almost

twenty years earlier in Mexico, for this was quite similar. It made the experience not quite so terrifying. On
one hand, I was thrilled to be experiencing this incredible energy. On the other, I wondered if I was simply
losing my mind.

I spent most of my time outside next to my pool
praying that I would make it through this experience
while waves of intense emotion washed through me
continuously. The first three days were so intense that I
was filled with wonder but also fear. After a week or so,
the energy seemed to mellow a bit, and I knew I would
survive. The intensification of energies and waves of
emotion also seemed to serve as a catalyst for a self-
evaluation of my life — my dreams, my purposes, my
goals. At times I felt tired, sluggish, irritable, frustrated,
and intensely emotional without being able to define a
cause. I was told through Joshua that emotion is one of
the tools through which drosses are removed from the
body, and that that was one of the purposes of the
emotion I was experiencing. In addition, he told me
that the polarities within my body were changing and
realigning, and that I was becoming more receptive —
more open to vibrational frequencies which were mani-
festing to a heightened degree on Mother Earth.

The Harmonic Convergence lasted approximately
one month for me. At the end of that month, I felt as
though I had been reborn on all levels. Overwhelmed
by the experience, I felt honored but also quite alone.
No one I knew at the time had felt anything occurring.

I felt so different — everything appeared changed.
The world was brighter, clearer. My mind was clear, my

body healthy and functioning perfectly. In spite of feeling so wonderful, at times I just wanted to have the "old me" back, to be "normal" again. I wondered if life would be easier, if I would have fewer problems. It soon became clear that this was not the case. In fact, the challenges in my life seemed to intensify; time seemed to have speeded up, with less breathing time between challenges. However, I seemed to see events in my life from a different perspective, as having distinct and clear purpose. Another result of my experience was giving up all alcohol. It seemed to have no place in my life anymore.

I felt strange sensations directly between my eyes in the sixth chakra or third eye — a vibration of sorts. I also found that my increased receptivity was a double-edged sword. I was, and still am, receptive to the highest and best, but also to those energies which I would rather not be receptive to. For example, when I went to one of my children's piano recitals and was sitting in the audience before the beginning of the program, I began to feel a very intense sensation of fear and quite sick to my stomach. I realized that I was actually feeling the nervousness of those waiting to perform. Even now, often shopping in malls or large grocery stores can be quite unpleasant for me as I feel the intensity of the emotions present. Shutting down my receptivity in such situations is something that I am still not completely successful with at times. Sometimes I simply forget to protect myself from intense energies, and I pay the price.

And ever since the Harmonic Convergence when I experience intense emotions personally, such as anger, physically I feel an intense heat permeating my body. If

I do not release this almost immediately through expression of the emotion and/or releasing it through meditation, I feel quite ill. Sometimes when a lot of emotion is released from a massage patient I am working with, I feel it in my body as heat, as if I have a high fever. Dealing with my receptivity has been an ongoing challenge. When Joshua was helping me to understand these many changes I was experiencing, he said that I had asked to be opened. Yes, I remember praying regularly to serve God in the highest and best way. But hey, I never asked for *this*!

Seeing a counselor, I wanted assurance that I was not crazy and not alone. She listened to my wild tale patiently but could not begin to relate to what I had gone through. Our three sessions together really didn't seem to accomplish anything, though I suppose just talking to someone was helpful. My husband and friends also listened patiently when I shared my experiences, but couldn't really relate, and I felt very alone until I received a reading on the Harmonic Convergence that Joshua had done.

The guides spoke about many of the things that I had experienced, and explained the Harmonic Convergence in the following way: "The Harmonic Convergence is perhaps the greatest of all opportunities which to this point in your Earth history has existed for you since the birth of the Master, the Christ, into your realms. The Convergence is simply to provide you with that wave, that crest of grace on which those of you who have entered the Earth plane to validate your worthiness as masters might have the opportunity of doing so,

to do so, and those of you, having done so, might through
the raising of the collective consciousness, raise the consciousness of the Earth plane at that time....

"Now it would seem that the vast majority of individuals within your sphere consider the entire matter
to be just as you stated it, moronic, that it has no meaning, that it's much ado about nothing.

"While they may walk within the darkness, it is im-
possible that their souls would not be touched by this
convergence in terms of the vibrational influence, in
terms of the blending or the harmonics of their souls'
energies into a force which can be acted upon by grace,
by the Law of Grace....

"The purpose for which many of you have entered
the earth plane (is) that you might accept your master-
ship and in doing so, might become aware of your di-
vine natures.... The earth has reached a level of growth
wherein this opportunity is being presented to you. It
is, in a manner of speaking, the triumph of the Forces
of Light over those which you know as the Forces of
Darkness.

"It will ultimately result in the battle between these
forces and the ultimate triumph of the Forces of Light.
In other words, the darkness, those forces contained
therein, shall at the conclusion or at the final wave or
crest of this convergence, be exterminated or overcome
by the Forces of Light, and there shall reign thereafter
1000 years of peace. It is the heralding of the birth of
the Master, the Christ, and it is the culmination in terms
of the life cycles of many souls within the earth.

"It is the culmination of work, of growth, by many

soul groupings and it provides the potential of the manifestation of the Christ consciousness within the earth plane once again.

"The Harmonic Convergence can be simply defined as the love of our Father which is grace in action. If there are areas of your life which you wish to change, if there are emotions which you wish to subdue, if there are behaviors which you wish to eliminate, if there are relationships which you wish to be refined or redefined, then now is the time to do it…."

In my journal on September 29th, 1987, about six weeks since the beginning of my Harmonic Convergence experience, I wrote: "I have gone through many changes physically — weird aches and pains, shifting of vertebrae, intense headaches, feeling out of sorts, etc. I feel I've been through most of it now. I feel a greater peace on all levels. Physically and on all levels, really, I feel wonderful. I have accepted the change I feel, and although it's very different, I am no longer threatened by feeling and being different. In fact, most of the time, I now realize this new reality is very beautiful, very special."

A few months after the Harmonic Convergence, I had a reading with a woman at a psychic fair. After a few minutes, she looked at me in amazement and asked, "*What* has happened to you? Every cell in your body is completely new!" I welcomed the validation that what I had experienced was real.

I also physically looked quite different. Those friends and family I saw daily did not seem to notice, but others commented on how young or rested I looked. One acquaintance I had not seen for a long time couldn't believe I was the same person, I looked so different. And of course, I wasn't the same person.

Chapter 6

## Releasing the Old

One of the major results of my Harmonic Convergence experience was a reassessment of my marriage. My husband and I had had many ups and downs in the fifteen years we had been married. A couple of years earlier, after a particularly difficult period and a decision to continue our commitment, my husband had given me a beautiful ruby ring for Valentine's Day. Soon after the Convergence, I noticed that the ring was broken. I couldn't imagine how the gold had split in half. I had been praying for guidance concerning my marriage, but not wanting to explore the obvious symbolism, I had the ring repaired.

Then in November of 1987, I had a dream I couldn't ignore. I was listening to a reading from Lama Sing in the dream, and I heard him say, "Yes, you do need to leave your marriage, but don't worry. Everything will be all right." I then experienced an incredible flooding of love throughout my being on all levels. Then I had the thought that Lama Sing couldn't interfere with my free will by telling me what to do, but I immediately said to myself, "But this is just a dream — he can tell me what to do in a dream."

Though I had been praying fervently for a clear message concerning my marriage, I was quite emotionally upset by the dream and didn't want to speak to my husband about it. Of course, he noticed my agitation, and when I told him about the dream, he couldn't believe that I would pay attention to a dream!

We went to a counselor together who turned out to be a born-again Christian who did not believe in divorce. He suggested my dream may have come from the devil. I remembered the incomparable feeling of love that I experienced during the dream and knew that the dream had been guidance from God.

Throughout this time, I was having constant pain in my right sacroiliac. Massages and chiropractic adjustments helped only temporarily. Through Joshua, I was told that in another lifetime during the Spanish Inquisition, I had not done what I knew to be right and was subsequently tortured on the rack. In fear for my own life, I had not come forward with information that could have saved someone else's life. The pain in my sacroiliac joint was a reminder that now, as in that lifetime, I was not following the light — not doing what I knew in my heart to be right for me.

My husband and our children did not want our marriage to end. I was so used to placing everyone else's needs and desires above my own, that following what I knew to be right for me by ending the marriage was one of the most difficult decisions of my life. When I finally ended the marriage, the pain in my sacroiliac magically disappeared completely.

We tend to cling tenaciously to that which is familiar, creating obstacles which inhibit change and growth; but I was finally ready to move ahead with my life.

Around this time, I began working with crystals as part of a Voyager Project. These beautiful "seeds of light," as Lama Sing refers to them, are valuable tools which store, transmit, focus, and amplify energies. I learned that having a crystal is similar to having a radio that is not tuned to a particular station. The crystal should be cleansed and then tuned to the person using the crystal and to a specific intent.

One way to cleanse crystals is by burying them in sea salt or placing them in a sea salt and water solution for a few days. The crystal is then carried on the person tuning the crystal for 10 days, allowing no one else to touch the crystal. During this time, meditate with the crystal nearby or in hand at least twice a day, morning and evening. On the evening of the tenth day, meditate for three consecutive days with the crystal on the solar plexus area, stating aloud three times the intent which the crystal will be attuned to. One which Lama Sing suggested and I used for many of my "seeds of light" was: "to attain a state of total joyfulness." The crystal then serves as a tool to draw those energies which contribute to this state and repel or filter out those energies which are not conducive to the desired state.

I used my crystals during my meditations and felt many energy shifts and positive effects as I struggled to maintain a sense of balance with my increased receptivity and the stress of going through a divorce. These friends from the mineral kingdom have assisted me in many times of need, and I also use them during my massage work.

Also around the time that my marriage was ending, I began studying polarity as an adjunct to massage therapy. Polarity balances the electromagnetic energy of the body, and is a wonderful healing tool. During one of the workshops I was attending, as I was working with someone, my heart began pounding wildly. When it subsided a few minutes later, I wondered if the woman I was working with was releasing fear during the treatment, and I was feeling it. A week or so later, I was told in a reading with Joshua that there was a master healer with one hand on my neck, the other on my heart, and that I would notice activity in my heart with his presence. His presence had caused the pounding heart I had experienced during the workshop. The pounding did not return. Instead, at times it felt as though my heart was doing little flip-flops inside my chest — almost like a baby moving inside when I was pregnant, but right in my heart! I alternated between wondering if I was crazy and feeling blessed that I had this guide with me, healing me and helping me to survive the tremendous stress of the divorce. It occurred to me that the sensations in my heart, so like the movements of new life within the womb, were signs of new life in my heart. By this time, I was getting quite used to very weird and unusual physical sensations.

These sensations in my heart have continued off and on for the past ten years, reminding me that I am never alone. They occur usually when I have taken the time to totally relax my body in preparation for meditation and many times when I am praying for healing. Having such a tangible sign that I am loved and that my companions in spirit are present always brings a smile to my heart and a great sense of peace and gratitude. Having an angel in my heart is a great gift!

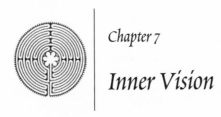

Chapter 7

## Inner Vision

*A*round the time of my divorce, I met a woman named Rachel who could see and read auras, the energy fields which surround every person. This gift had manifested after the death of one of her sons. Through her psychic readings and a course she taught, Rachel assisted me on my spiritual path and in my personal growth.

Before I had met Rachel, at times during my meditations I would reach a point when I would experience tremendous fear. My heart would pound intensely, and I would have to end my meditation. Rachel saw during a reading that I had actually left my body during one lifetime while in meditation and was unable to return. The subconscious memory of this death made me afraid to move beyond a certain point in my meditations. Since that reading, that fear has totally disappeared, and I no longer experience such a reaction.

Rachel also helped me to understand the following experience: One day while at the beach with a male friend, I had the overwhelming urge to hug him, my heart pressed against his. I apologized as I clung to him tightly, explaining that I didn't know why I had to hug him, but I did. After ten or fifteen minutes, I released him and realized that an energy imbalance I had been experiencing for some time had disappeared, and I once again felt healthy and grounded. During my next reading with Rachel, she told me that I had been given a valuable tool for balancing my electromagnetic energies. I had experienced a polarity treatment of sorts as I hugged my male friend. It was possible to balance myself by imagining and feeling energy flowing from my heart to the male's heart, moving from his heart down to his first chakra (in the area of the coccyx), passing from his first chakra to mine, and then moving up my body, returning once again to my heart chakra. I have used this method of balancing my electromagnetic energies many times with usually great success.

Rachel's class, aptly named InnerVision, assisted those in the small class to develop their intuitive abilities. We studied the chakras, or energy centers, of the body and practiced "reading" each other's chakras. I have never been a very visual person, so while many in the class had visions or images relating to the chakras of the subject, I more often tended to pick up feelings or sensations.

During our last class, Rachel played seven different pieces of music, one for each major chakra, and we were to tune into each of our own chakras, recording our experiences by writing.

As I tuned into my chakras, I received several images and then began to hear words, or messages, as though my guides or my own Higher Self was speaking to me. When I reached my fourth, or heart chakra, I sensed pure love flowing to me and through me on all levels. I wrote rapidly as I received this message: "Love thyself. Thou art beautiful. Thou art God. All things are yours. Love thy neighbor. Share your great gifts of wisdom and love. Be love, give love. You are love. Let your love touch every corner of the Earth, the universe. You are pure love, as every other being on this planet. Many may not know it. Help others to see the love, the beauty within themselves. Guide them, love them, show them the way.

"Share your experience, your knowledge, your beauty. This is truly loving. Love God through loving yourself. You are ONE. Be it. Know it. Live it. Let joy be your way of life. (The tears were now flowing freely, running down my cheeks.) The tears falling are tears for all the times you have not loved yourself. Release totally. Love totally."

As Rachel changed the music for the fifth, or throat chakra, I heard: "Don't be afraid to share your gifts, your knowledge. Others will benefit from your opening. This is your purpose. You are here to help others, to share with others — yourself, your experiences, your love. Open up. Never be afraid again to express yourself, your truth. You have so much to give, to speak. You can be a light unto the world."

As the music was changed once again, I tuned into my sixth or third eye or brow chakra, and saw an image of a flower, fully formed, fully open. God's nectar was flowing down from above, radiating down to all levels. I heard "flowing freely, smoothly, in accordance with thy spirit, God's will — which are one. Trust, trust the information. Know that you are at one with His will. You will feel it. You will know it."

As the music was changed for the final time, I focused on the seventh and last chakra, the crown chakra; I heard: "You and I are One. Know it. Live it. Feel the joy of being God. All things that I am, you are. My energy is your energy. My joy is your joy. Follow me all the days of your life, and you shall dwell in the house of the Lord forever." Then I heard my Higher Self speaking to myself: "I am loved. I am a vessel of Thy love. This love flows all the way down through my centers, back up and out into the world and all of existence."

This was my first experience with what may be termed automatic writing. I heard my guides, my Higher Self, or God — I didn't know which or if it had been all three — speaking directly to me. I was overwhelmed by the love with which I was being blessed.

To develop this gift of automatic writing, I began to tune into some of my massage patients before their appointments. I would, as Rachel had taught me, mentally cleanse the room where I was doing the reading with a beautiful sphere of white light. After the light had picked up all errant energy, I would release the light and the energy to God. Grounding myself deep into Mother Earth, then I moved my consciousness into my "reading space," which is physically located behind the third eye. After prayers of protection and asking that only the highest forces of love and truth surround the reading, I asked the patients' Higher Selves to tell my Higher Self whatever they needed to hear to assist them on their path at the present time. I then would receive a message which I would record in writing. Channeling this guidance was quite enjoyable for me. I felt tremendous love flowing through me to the recipient of the information, and I was told by my patients that the readings were very helpful and relevant. Soon I began doing readings for friends and acquaintances. I was even paid for some of my efforts. This was fun, and I was once again the magician!

During this time, I traveled with a friend to Virginia Beach to visit the Edgar Cayce Foundation. After attending a lecture on psychic dreams, that night I dreamed that Rachel told me that she had been told that I was going to be psychic, and that my guides would bring me to her to learn things. I had the sense this would be "out of body." I would be flown to her. I saw myself being carried on someone's hip as we flew, cradled by an arm, like I sometimes used to carry my children when they were babies.

While there in Virginia Beach, I met Joshua for the first time. And around the same time I also had the op-

portunity to meet Al, the channel for Lama Sing, at a
Be Your Own Psychic symposium in Ft. Myers, Florida.
It was wonderful to connect the faces to those voices
which brought me the messages of my guides. When I
finally met Al, I had had my first reading with Lama
Sing eleven years earlier.

Perhaps the most valuable lesson in meeting and
being present in the physical with these people who
were the channels of most of my spiritual education
was the realization that they were just as human as I,
with problems and challenges in their lives just like me
and all of my brothers and sisters in the Earth. There
was the tendency, especially before meeting these gifted
channels in person, to place them on a pedestal, to think
of them as almost superhuman, to believe that somehow they were above me or better than I was. They had
beautiful gifts which they were using with the highest
intents and purposes. The truth is that we are all uniquely
gifted. We have but to discover these gifts, acknowledge
them, and use them in the highest and best way. Each
of our gifts is just as beautiful as another's. And no one
is closer to God than another. We are all a part of All
That Is. It is a matter of believing it, knowing it, living
it, and opening up to the love which we already are.

I did not have the opportunity to study with Rachel
for very long. I dreamed that she and her husband were
getting divorced. This did come to pass, and I was heart-
broken when she told me she was moving on. All of my
previous spiritual teachers were guides in other realms
whose teachings were channeled during the readings I
had received. Rachel was the first teacher I could reach

out and touch in the physical world. It was difficult to let her go.

Joshua had said of Rachel: "The entity is intended to teach. You must take the very best that she has to offer, and then when you reach a point wherein you believe you can go no further, or you believe you have gained the maximum levels of information which are available, then you must be ready to move forward." Another lesson in letting go.

Chapter 8

# Shamanic Journeys

*I* n July of 1989 when I was almost forty years old,
my companions in spirit, as given through Lama
Sing, provided me with a view of Robin: "The entity
Robin is having a dream. In this dream, she is a female
entity in the Earth. She is at a point which is abundant
in interaction with others. In these interactions, she finds
that the experiences are not those which she would
choose, that entities are making choices and having actions which are not in accordance with what she knows
to be best. And yet there seems to be the inability to

guide, to direct, or to even demonstrate why these paths are errant or not the best.

"There is the effort on the part of the entity Robin to reach out and to embrace others in this dream. And as she does so, she sees that they may for a moment here or there return that embrace so as it fulfills their need or expectation in that time. And then they for one reason or another may move on; or she may choose to move on. And in all of this, as Robin has this dream, there can be seen the desire for something which is consistent and which is a source of joy and abundance for her. All the while, Robin looks for this here and there and in the presence of others and other relationships. We can see that she already has what she seeks.

"The question is then, dear entity Robin, how long will you look outside of self for that which you already have? If you turn back from this, back to life and to look again to fulfill yourself in the manner which has become your habit — or perhaps more appropriately, that which is your expectation — then how can that which is within be truly realized and become a part of your life if you turn from it to look for that outside of self?

"Fulfill self. Grasp the abundance and the potential within your own being completely. Embrace it. Surround yourself with it. Have faith, and from that faith, let joy be your outer countenance. Be fluid, be flexible. Move and act in accordance with that guidance as you test it and know it to be correct in accordance with the Law Universal. But as you would shirk from this, tempted or drawn by a sense of loneliness or emptiness in the outer sense, then the best is left behind in search for something which can never be as complete as this. See?

"Once that completeness has been borne into your life totally, that you might become as called "born again," then so is this awakening as a rebirth, and then you will attract and will be attracted to that which is the best, which will only maximize or amplify what you already have. If you go forward in the sense of being lacking or limited, then you shall sow the seeds. You cannot fulfill yourself through the presence of another. You can only amplify your own fulfillment by their presence through sharing it. In other words, gain the fulfillment which is within, and let this be amplified by associations with others. See?"

At the time I received that reading, I had just experienced a very devastating romantic relationship. I learned from that relationship to honor myself by not allowing a man in my life who did not honor and respect me. Extremely fragile, I was suffering deeply from a broken heart. I took a trip to Hawaii — for the sun, sand, and sea have always been great healers for me. Driving alone to the top of Mt. Haleakala on Maui, just before the end of my drive, I looked out over the stark, treeless landscape. Perched atop a rock in the middle of the afternoon, sat an owl staring directly at me. I did a double-take, not believing my eyes. The owl was so surreal, not belonging in that place at that time. This was my first spirit visitation in animal form. Owl symbolizes wisdom. The owl came to commend me for the wisdom I had gained as a result of that extremely painful relationship. I had learned my lessons well.

So often here on Mother Earth we choose to learn

our lessons through pain, for pain is not easily forgotten. Hawaii is such a magical, healing place. My energies were renewed as a result of that trip, and I looked forward to the next adventure. After my return from Hawaii, I wrote this poem as an expression of my feelings of oneness with the universe and the Creator:

Not a footprint on the beach,
The white sand slithers
Like smoke across my path
Stinging my legs.
Such joy in solitude!

I open my heart
To the wind, to the salty spray,
And I feel You
Walking beside me, inside of me,
Reminding me we are One.

Later that year, on New Year's Eve of 1989, I had a beautiful vision during my mediation. Many mountain peaks rose above a sea of white clouds. A voice told me, "You will experience new and wondrous things." I was filled with gratitude. And what a year that was to be!

Having read about a shaman named Brant Secunda in *Yoga Journal* magazine, I attended a seminar that summer with him at Feathered Pipe Ranch outside of Helena, Montana. Brant was an American who had lived and apprenticed with a Mexican Huichol Indian shaman, Don Jose Matsuwa, for twelve years. Don Jose had sent Brant out into the world to teach the ancient

Huichol Indian healing and purification techniques. The singing, the dancing, the drumming, the prayer circles spoke to my heart and stirred memories of other lifetimes.

Brant helps to support the Huichols by selling many of their beautiful works of art, including yarn paintings, during his seminars. These "paintings" are wonderful depictions of shamanic visions in brilliant, vivid color. They are created by "dreaming shamans" by pressing many colors of yarn, strand by strand, onto a wooden surface covered by a thin layer of beeswax. Two of the yarn paintings displayed side by side on a ledge in the lodge at Feathered Pipe Ranch had caught my attention, and I was having difficulty deciding which one to purchase. As I stood admiring them both, they both leaped off the ledge at exactly the same moment, landing with a very loud bang, face up, on a table below the ledge. Moved by the magic, I bought them both.

Invited by Brant to join his gathering at Mt. Rainier near Seattle less than a week later, I flew home to Florida. Then, impulsively, with two of my children, I flew back across the country to Seattle. As I looked out the window of the airplane just before landing, I saw mountain peaks poking above a layer of clouds, just as I had in my vision!

As Brant spoke in our circles about honoring all of life and taught us ancient Huichol ceremonies, I noticed a change in my son. The divorce had been an extremely difficult, confusing time for him, and he seemed to see no meaning or purpose in life. But he seemed changed by his experience on Mt. Rainier, as if through Brant's teachings, he had glimpsed a glimmer of hope that life was more than the pain and suffering he was experiencing.

After the workshop, we drove to the airport in Portland, Oregon, to pick up my older daughter, who was joining us there. We drove through Oregon and California, stopping and enjoying the magnificent redwoods on the way. We stayed in San Francisco a few days, then flew home to Florida. It was an impulsive, spur-of-the-moment trip which was a great and enjoyable adventure. We had all suffered through the divorce, and it was a much needed time of togetherness and fun.

Soon after our return, I had another vision during one of my meditations. I saw a friend of mine, who had one daughter and was pregnant at the time, seated with two children. On one side was her daughter, and on the other a young son. I called her and asked if she knew the sex of her baby yet. She said she expected to know the next day when she received the results of some tests. Telling her about my vision, I told her I believed that she would have a son. The next day she called to say I was correct.

I was continuing to do readings for others through automatic writing and also enjoyed getting intuitive messages outside of those readings. Every day was a new adventure, and I looked forward to the changes Lama Sing had spoken about in a recent reading: "Changes are yet ahead, and many of these changes shall come about abruptly and with no forewarning. Some of the opportunities should be looked for just in the same way — suddenly upon you as unique opportunities which may make one day separated from the other seem like two different lifetimes. If your attitude is joyful and anticipatory and positive, you will meet those opportunities and gain and be fruitful as the result. Do not expend any significant amount of time in frustration or lamentation over that which has gone before. Look to the now, look to the future, and contribute to self in the Earth equally as you would to the spiritual and mental self."

Chapter 9

## The Magic of Merlin

*J* had my first meeting with the wizard, Merlin, in November of 1990. A friend had told me that I should have a reading with a woman named Diana who channeled Merlin. She lived in California and did readings over the phone. I ignored the suggestion for a number of months, feeling that I had plenty of guidance from my readings with Al and Joshua. But Merlin kept knocking on the door of my thoughts, so to speak, and I made an appointment for a reading. At the appointed time, I called, not having any idea what to expect.

After some prayers and toning by Diana, I was greeted by Merlin: "Good day. Blessings to you, my sweet.

It is I, one who is termed Master Merlin, who comes to chat with you, to bring you some, what you would term, expanded consciousness, and to tickle your little fancy, here and there, to make you laugh and love and to re-member — to remember that which you are.

"Now. My dear child, you have been on this path for quite some time, not just in this lifetime, but lifetime after lifetime. And we are very pleased to be able to connect with you again, for I will say to you that you are familiar with my vibration. I am one who is termed the wizard, hmmm?, one who has worked with planet Earth for a very, very long time.

"Now. I want you to recall a land which I am going to term the Land of Nod. It is a land which is some-place in between what I will term the third and fourth dimension — a place that one might go if they were aligned and awakened — something like 3.5, if you will, dimension, a land that existed beyond the mists and in another reality. I would like to take you to that land today for just awhile, for there is going to be activation of your energy field. And there is going to be activation of cer-tain codes of remembrance, which are part of your ac-tual DNA structure.

"And so it is that I would ask you to begin now to enter into a very deep state of relaxation and to become adjusted now to the frequencies and the alignments which we are sending to you. I have called forth, into your vicinity, three angelic beings which shall stand guard, appropriately, as we do this work. You have been preparing for such an initiation for quite some time and, if you are willing to proceed, we will proceed now. (I asked, "Should I lie down?") If you can, it would be most helpful.

"Now. I would like you to begin simply by breathing in that color which I will term the cobalt blue. Just breathe it in and allow yourself to become very relaxed, very comfortable; don't worry about what you hear or don't hear, but rather just let this experience occur. For you will have this on the tape, as it is termed, and you can listen more specifically later.

"At this point, I am to call forth now the energies of what I am going to term a light vehicle, that which is termed the Merkaba. This is a pyramidal structure that we are going to place above you and below you, so that, in a sense, you are in the middle of a diamond shape. And I want to station these angels about this to begin to bring about heightened energy force fields all around you.

"Now. There are three centers which we are going to work upon today — that being the third eye, that being the throat, and that being the heart. We are going to work on removing certain seals and activating certain codes that you carried with you into this planetary existence.

"Now. As we begin to shift the energy field, you will, perhaps, sense some changing in the light vibrations around you, for we are bringing in at this time a very powerful white and gold frequency that is going to surround you during this entire, what I will term, operation.

"Now. You are an old surgeon, hummm?, of the light and, one might say, so am I. In another reality we would term it simply alchemy — the ability to change one's perception and therefore change one's reality. As you continue to focus upon relaxing, there will be many shifts in your own structure, which is activated.

"Now. We are going to ask that the inter-dimensional doorways be opened to the fourth and to the fifth dimensions. And at the same time we are going to ask that the inter-dimensional doorways be opened to the second and the first dimensions, and that there be created a window, a very powerful window, which we shall weave with the fabric of light and that you are now inside of this window. I would like you to visualize at this time that you are lying upon a very large and brilliantly green crystal — like a crystal bed. And this green is a green that would be termed both emerald and neon at the same time. And I would like you to imagine that the crystal has been, in a sense, carved out so that there is a body form that you can actually lie down in and be very comfortable in.

"Now. I am going to call forth now the energies of the alter-aspect of creation and ask that it begin to beam frequencies of very powerful light into all of your chakras at this time to create a balancing and a healing for you. As we scan your chakras, we see that there has been some damage done both to the first and the second chakras, which we will repair at this time, the first chakra having to do with a sense of insecurity that you have had a great deal of your life — a sense of, perhaps, not belonging or not being accepted. Now, we ask the hands of light to come forward at this time and to repair this area and to infuse it with, what we will term, a red and gold vibration. (I began to feel a lot of heat in the area of my first chakra.)

"Now. You have been stuck in a pattern for a very long time of being somewhat afraid to move forward — to, in a sense, take risks. Although you do take risks, it is not a pleasant . . . step that you look forward to. As we energize and we weave the walls of this chakra, you will find that you will have less hesitancy and less fear in moving forward and committing fully your life to the golden light.

"Now. We are going to place a seal of protection into this chakra, and this is coming from a very high aspect of creation. And we would remind you at this point of your angelic heritage. We would remind you of your connection with those whom we will term the angels, and know that you have traveled with them and that you have been among their ranks. And that you very much still are in communication with the angelic forces. It may be subtle, but nonetheless it is there. And so, as we place this seal, there will be a remembrance, and you will feel the protection that is always about you.

"Now. Continue to feel the healing vibration of this powerful green altar crystal. And we shall move up to the second chakra where, again, there has been a great deal of damage, so to speak. We are going to lift from that area some patterns and memories that are very old, indeed. We are perceiving here some, ehhh, remem-brances of lifetimes of slavery in that which is termed Egypt. And we wish for you to release yourself from the bondage of the slavery and from the consciousness of slavery, and also to release yourself from the anger at those who would create slavery and bondage, and know that in your existence you have been in both positions, both as the slave and as the master.

"Now. In this lifetime you have somewhat of, what I will term, an overlay of consciousness in relation to men in that oftentimes you feel as if there is a bondage which occurs in relationships. So, at this time, we will fill this center and we weave these tears and rips in the walls of the chakra and bring forth the gold and orange and yellow vibration to fill this hollow space.

"You are to let go of this concept — that men will place you in bondage. You see, part of it is just your feeling, at one level, that just coming to Earth is being placed in bondage, for you are very high souled, your spirit is very evolved, and for you to descend into the layers, into this lifespace, in a sense, is as a bondage. And somehow you have projected it out into relationships, which has caused you to have many incarnations in slavery and being the one who creates bondage. So it is time to undo this knot and to just allow it to be lifted by the hands of light from your being. Good. We are making fabulous progress here.

"Now. We are going to move up to the solar plexus. This is a real point of power for you. This is a point of impact — whether you are impacted upon or whether you impact your environment. There is some armoring upon this place, upon your body, in the solar plexus. And underneath that armoring is the anger, so to speak, about being in bondage. So, we are going to place a very powerful vibration of a green and a violet hue to begin to break up that armoring so that you can trust your environment, and you can begin to trust going out into the world, and you can begin to trust that relationship is possible on an equal basis — not where one partner is dominating and one partner is being dominated. So as we bring forth the blue, the green, the violet, begin to harmonize this area. (My eyes closed, I saw these colors as Merlin spoke of them.) You will feel a release, a shift, a change in your belief systems.

"Now. In this particular area, in the solar plexus, there are some very powerful remembrances — other lifetimes, if you will, other time frames, if you will — in which you have been fully cognizant of your powers and of your beliefs in the light and in your magnificence. I want to activate those particular coded memories in that area, that you can begin to believe in yourself at a much deeper level, and believe that you can have an impact on your world and believe that you are an emissary of the light. And I would also like to activate that, which I will term, your contract for this incarnation. It is no mistake that you have come to us at this point in time to receive these activations. It is truly what you have been searching for.

"Now. This is going to awaken also memories of times when you have been involved in lifetimes, one in particular, with that being which is termed Moses. We would very much like you to remember your connection and your loyalty and your friendship with this one who is termed, Moses. There is within you also a remembrance of the tablets, as they are termed, and the correct reading of the tablets. As we activate this memory, you will find that in your healing work, this informa-

tion of the correct understanding and reading and perception of the tablets will begin to flow directly through
your channels into those whom you are working upon.
Good.

"We are going to move now to the heart chakra.
This is a point of very great concern at this time. And
the reason that I say this is that you are carrying some
very valuable possibilities with you — possibilities to
actually shift the consciousness of others as you work
with them. Just as we are at this time actually shifting
your consciousness, this capability can and, perhaps, will
be activated in you.

"Now. As we pierce the heart chakra, we are going
to lift the veils, the dimensional doors, as they are termed.
If you remember, we asked for the releasing of the guard-
ianship from the first dimension to the fifth, and I will
explain to you a little bit more, later, exactly what that
means.

"In the heart chakra, there have been planted what
we will term original seeds of discontent. Imagine, if
you will, that there was such a place as the Garden of
Eden. Just imagine we are speaking metaphorically. And
imagine that that garden was most beautiful when along
came that which we will term a darkened force, which
decided to plant seeds of discontent. There are those who,
from time to time, will descend to the planet and who
will take upon themselves the seed of discontent, who
will carry it in the hopes of transmuting a lot of that
energy. In this heart center, then, exists one of these seeds
of discontent, and it exists at the first dimensional level,
which is basically your tie into the human psyche, into

the mass human psyche.

"Now, my sweet one. We would like you to imagine, if you will, that you are lying in the middle of a great window and that there is a great light coming from that which is termed the office of the Christ, or the Christ consciousness, from the fifth dimension, through the fourth, through you in the third, down into the second, deep into the heart and into the first dimension of consciousness. And we are going to begin to let the light of that Christ consciousness flow and begin to release this seed of discontent through you.

"Now. There has been a gripping in the heart — almost as if there is some other reason than you know, why it is that you cannot fully trust, why it is that you fully cannot allow yourself to be who you are. You have taken on the seed of discontent and what it is, is a separation of mankind from God. You have been carrying a portion of this seed in your heart for a very long time, and the prayer work and the intense love that you have and the powerful dedication that you have always had is also attempting to release this seed of discontent.

"As you allow these veils to be pierced with the light, we will say to you that we are very grateful for your carrying this particular seed and that you are now to release it into the light and allow it to be removed from you, from the consciousness of mankind, forever.

"This has to do with some activation of some memory in Atlantis, memory of a time when you were actively involved in creating your future consciousness. In other words, there was a procedure in which you could project yourself into the future to this point in

time and where you could plan, so to speak, our meeting and the removal of this seed of discontent. We are
going to infuse this area with a great violet and pink
light, and we are going to encase it in gold. (Once again
I saw the colors as Merlin spoke of them.) And your
memories and your energy system will begin to shift
dramatically. So be it.

"Now. We are going to move into the throat. Let the
throat recognize its value. Let the throat recognize its
creativity, its power, its purpose. This is an area of great
and deep understanding, the throat chakra, and it ties in
directly to your commitment to being on this planet,
for this is your area of expression. And what we would
simply do, in this area, is to place in there an image of
the angelic ones whom you have walked with, so that
your expression will begin to consciously carry this
vibratory frequency of the angels. We would like you to
see choirs and choirs and choirs of the angels, and we
would like you to see yourself stepping from those ranks
— stepping forward and kneeling before that one which
we term Michael, and having his sword placed upon your
shoulders and upon your forehead as you prepare to
come forth and to lend your hand and your heart and
your being to the healing of mankind. And we also seal
this now in the gold and the violet light. (I saw these
things happening as Merlin described them.)

"Moving into the third eye area — blessed being,
you have drawn quite a veil over this — perhaps for
your own protection, perhaps so others would not truly
recognize you. We are going to ask now the hands of
light to remove some of these veils and to begin to

activate and stimulate the pineal gland and the pituitary gland, not to overstimulate — just to stimulate — and to reset, as it would be termed, the frequency. You see, as these two glands are awakened or stimulated, if you will, they release certain chemical vibrations into the bloodstream which will begin to activate codes which you carry — healing codes, consciousness codes. You are doing very well, very well.

"As I look into this area, I see a great deal of confusion in the sense that what you saw with your third eye did not match what you were seeing, so to speak, with your physical eyes; that the world of the true reality of the third eye did not match what was being said to you or the messages that you were receiving from others. This caused you a lot of confusion in your childhood. And so, at a very early age, we would say that you shut down, as it were, what would be termed your higher abilities. Nonetheless, you have retained a very powerful connection with God. That light has been like a beacon for you, guiding you and directing you. What we do this day is to bring forth the consciousness into your being that you have very powerful vision, that which you would term clairvoyant vision — very powerful — and that, over time, you will begin to use it more and more and more. What we are doing today is removing a veil and stimulating that center. We are also going to place a new seal within this chakra, and this seal is perhaps what one might term a channeling seal — channeling, in the sense of receiving more clearly telepathic messages, pictures, ideas. You have asked to be more aligned with your guidance. This seal is coming forth also from the office of the Christ and is, indeed, activated much at the cellular level. We are very pleased to have you receive this beautiful vibration. It is time.

"Now, for the crown — that beautiful, vibrating flower of life. As we look upon this area, we see what we might term some sadness or some regret, if you will — some beliefs in sadness and beliefs in regret. We are going to cleanse this area for you, and we are going to bring about some new patterns, patterns which are more aligned with your highest truth. We would like you to envision at this time the archangels, Gabriel and Michael, to see their auric field, see the light about them and to visualize, if you will, the corona — that which might be termed a halo that exists on the very outer edges of their auras. (I saw Gabriel and Michael and their coronas.)

"We would like you to remember what it is to have a corona and to allow the corona to be that which is termed a transmutation fire, and all those thoughts which clutter the crown chakra are now being consumed by that transmutation fire. You have many worries that you plague yourself with, and they are cluttering up your true ability to be aligned with true power. We are going to place a corona of light around the outside of your aura and ask that it begin to draw off and release and transmute any toxic thoughts that exist in and around you. And upon the very tip top of the crown chakra, we are going to place the emblem and the seal of the eagle. You can allow that now to begin to interface with the rest of your vibrations.

"Now my sweet one. The initiation has been completed. There has been extreme activation. You will feel many shifts and changes over the next several weeks' time, preparing you for that moment which is termed the winter solstice and that moment which is termed the Christmas Eve. Those are going to be very important days or, shall I say, nights for you this year. They will be symbolic rites of passage into a new era, into a new chapter of your life and of your existence. So in the next six to seven weeks' time, you will want to be, as it were, more quiet than usual, a bit more introspective, and just begin to listen and observe the changes that will be occurring. All of the work and the dedication and the preparation have brought you to this point to be able to step through to this new level of initiation.

"Now. I would like you to begin to breathe deeply, to breathe into yourself a golden yellow light. (I saw the light filling my being.) And we will begin now to release the dimensional doors and ask that you be sealed in a vibration of protection and in a vibration of sacred acceptance. And we will now release the hands of light, giving thanks to the alter-vibration for coming forth to do this surgery. Releasing now the inter-dimensional Merkaba, releasing you now from the green crystal, and bringing you back now into this third dimensional reality.

"Continue to breathe deeply. We will ask the three angels who have come to stay with you to help stabilize this energy and to allow you to go into deep states of rest when you need to.

"Things will be different, my dear one. Things will be very different. You will feel it slowly over the next few months' time. And by that which is termed the New

Year, there will be a great more stability and balance and strength in your life. Opportunities will begin to show themselves. New doors will begin to open, and your ability to discern a direction will be much more powerful. You will not fluctuate so much as you have in the past — not so much fluctuation, not at all. Your path has been more illumined, and your feet will be grounded into that which is the true path. So.

"This is quite an extraordinary reading, as it is termed, for it has not been a reading at all. It has been an acceleration and an initiation. And that is why we have been called forth into your path. As I have said, it was pre-ordained and pre-understood that it would happen. And you, in fact, designed it long ago for this moment in time. So.

"I shall begin now to release the channel. As you begin now to move your fingers and toes and begin to come back to, oh, perhaps feeling rested, alert — feeling courageous, strong, and feeling that you know that you know. So.

"My blessings to you, child, and I shall be on my way. So be it and so it is. We ask that this shall be sealed, recorded and given forth into the proper hands of light. Blessings now. So be it."

As I hung up the phone, I felt as though I was almost in a state of shock. I didn't know if what I had experienced was real. Part of me believed that something very exciting and significant had truly just occurred. Another part of me thought that it couldn't have been real — I didn't know the first thing about Diana or whether an energy known as Merlin truly existed. I decided to wait and see if I felt the changes I had been told would occur. I felt quite strange physically, much different than I had before the phone call, and wondered if I was just getting sick. I knew time would tell.

During the next week, I felt like a different person. As after my Harmonic Convergence experience, I felt cleansed, reborn. I slept a lot. Still wondering if I was just crazy, I had a reading with Joshua who was in town visiting a friend. I had not told him about the initiation with Merlin.

As I walked into the room, Joshua commented that I had a six-pointed star in the middle of my aura. Then as he began the reading, he told me that one of my guides was handing me a white rose. She told me through Joshua that I had been married into a brotherhood of those who had asked to serve, and that I should look for signs of confirmation that what I had heard and was feeling was true. My guides recommended that I meditate regularly and at 2 a.m. if possible. Asking what it had meant to have the seal of the eagle placed upon the tip of my crown chakra, I was told that that signified mastering the heart and balancing the upper centers with the lower centers. This all sounded very exciting to me, but I wasn't aware of accomplishing any of this!

I was very curious about what was to occur during the winter solstice and Christmas Eve. My guides wanted Joshua to tell me that that would be the birth, the real birth of the light within me. The last message they gave me was that if I had any questions, anything I needed help with, I was "to meditate and ask, believe, and accept."

My ability to believe that all of these incredible things were truly happening was stretched to the limit. At times I felt that I had definitely gone off the deep end. Everywhere I went, I saw symbols of the eagle. Signs outside of churches referred to Moses. On the counter as I was paying for something at a store, I saw a checkbook cover with a beautiful painting of the magician Merlin at work. Merlin's spirit is very much alive and present in the town where I live now, and there is even a town nearby known as Merlin, but in Florida at that time I had never seen any sign of Merlin anywhere.

Just two weeks after my initiation with Merlin, I left for a workshop with Brant near Puerto Vallerta, Mexico. By that time, I had absolutely no doubt that the initiation was real — strange, but real. I had felt totally different since that day — my energy was very heightened, and I felt quite aligned and balanced on all levels. There were periods when I felt the need to totally withdraw from everything and just rest. Meditating more often and more deeply, I felt wonderful. I had an overwhelming sense of gratitude and love for my spirit guides, for my Creator, for my life. I allowed myself to feel great love for myself for allowing it all to happen.

Chapter 10

## Mexico

*T*he workshop I attended with Brant in Puerto
Vallarta inspired me to write the following poem:

Oh Grandmother Ocean, the sound of your waves
Breaking upon the shore
Carries me to that place
Of harmony, joy, and peace evermore.

From which we came —
That center of radiating light
To which I long to return;
I look within and see it shining brightly.

## The Magic of Dreams and Spirit Guides

As the moon upon the ocean
Lights up the deepest night,
The eternal flame within my heart
Guides my steps with love and light.

Grandfather Fire, take me to your sacred heart,
Grandmother Ocean, take me to your greatest depths
Of love, of truth and compassion.
Oh Mother Earth, never let me feel apart.

Let me take the time each and every day
To honor all of life both great and small.
For there, Great Spirit, I will find You
In every living thing I meet today.

Oh Father Sun, your warmth will melt
The greatest anger, fear, and sadness
And replace them with the most precious love
This humble heart has ever felt.

Don Jose, Brant's beloved teacher and adopted grandfather, had died not long before our gathering in Mexico.
One morning as Brant spoke in the circle, he told us of
a dream the night before in which Don Jose had hugged
him, and my tears began to flow. I missed my own sweet
father terribly, and wished that he would visit me in my
dreams. It had been a long time. Dad heard my silent
prayer and visited me the next night. He looked just as
he had when he left for the spirit world. Giving me a
hug, he told me he was teaching psychology to those on
the other side and working with the elderly of the Earth.

He told me he needed to be careful about what colors he wore, or they could see him. It was so wonderful to see him again, and when it was time for him to leave, I watched him fly up a staircase and out the window. I had a good cry when I awoke.

Everything was so wonderful and magical. I probably even began to feel a little bit special — such incredible things had happened. Well, that didn't last long! To my horror, I discovered that I had picked up something in Mexico I hadn't expected, presumably from a toilet seat. A case of Montezuma's revenge would have been much preferred over this nasty surprise! I couldn't believe this was happening to me.

Shocked and embarrassed, I asked in my meditation why this had happened. I heard, "Don't sweat the small stuff." At the time of course, it wasn't "small stuff" from my perspective. But I did get the message clearly — in spite of my magical experiences, I was still in and of the Earth and had to deal with all that that involved. I didn't suffer from delusions of being "special" again.

A few days later Brant was performing a healing in the center of the circle. Behind him and the woman receiving the healing appeared a huge white bird, taller than a human. It didn't look like a real bird to me, but rather half human, half bird — resembling a bird but standing upright as a human does. As I blinked and rubbed my eyes, the spirit disappeared. I knew that Brant called on the spirits during his healings, but it was wonderful to witness the presence of one myself.

And I was again reminded of the love, support, and presence of my companions in spirit one morning as I meditated at 4 a.m. I had the unmistakable sensation of someone holding each of my hands in theirs.

Later, as Brant performed a ceremony to honor and welcome the time of the coming winter solstice, I was quite curious as to what lay ahead for me on that day and on Christmas Eve.

*Chapter 11*

# Rites of Passage

*M*erlin and my other guides had really not given me any idea of what to expect on the winter solstice. I had learned that for the Huichols and other native peoples of Mother Earth, winter is the time for going within. It seemed appropriate that, for me, it would be the time of the birth of the light within. But what exactly did that mean? I imagined it would be an event more beautiful than any I had ever experienced. Perhaps my guides and angels would even appear to me!

Upon my return from the Mexican trip, I felt that I should know the exact time of the winter solstice. Calling an astrologer friend, I was told it would occur at

10:07 p.m. on the appointed day. On December 21st, alone in the house, I listened to a Lama Sing tape as I waited for the big event. Feeling a bit weird, I told myself there was nothing to fear. I considered the possibility of experiencing nothing and finding out that it was all a silly dream.

At 10:07, I began to feel quite ill. Nauseated, shaking, shivering, and having chills, I wondered if I had food poisoning. Having fantasies of checking myself into a hospital, I spent a while in the bathroom as my bowels emptied. Extremely upset that food poisoning was causing me to miss out on experiencing the birth of the light (whatever that was), I felt very strange and dizzy and noticed a feeling of energy beginning in my first chakra and moving up. There was a lot of activity occurring in my intestines and stomach, causing loud gurgling sounds and a feeling of queasiness. Chills and rushes wracked my body, and I felt very cold and weak — almost as though my body had turned to jelly and was quivering all over. Returning to the bedroom, I tried to ignore the discomfort in my body and continued to listen to the Lama Sing tape. I noticed that the energy had moved up to my throat.

Almost exactly one hour after the onset of the illness, all the symptoms disappeared as suddenly as they had appeared, and I felt wonderful and quite energized. I laughed at myself, realizing that the physical "illness" I had experienced was obviously my rite of passage. This realization left me feeling quite confused and a bit disappointed. Well, there was still Christmas Eve to look forward to. Perhaps the second of my rites of passage would be more enlightening or at least more enjoyable!

The children and I left the next day to celebrate Christmas with my family in St. Petersburg, Florida. Walking along the beach there, I felt a profound sense of peace and gratitude, which I expressed with these words:

Good morning, seagull!
Thank you for brightening my day with your flight.
Good morning, children!
Thank you for filling my ears with your laughter.
Good morning, glistening waters!
Thank you for putting a sparkle into my step.
Good morning, God and guardian angels!
Thank you for illuminating this day and my heart
with joy and wonder and love.

On Christmas Eve day, I awoke looking forward to my final rite of passage. Unlike the winter solstice, I had no idea of exactly when to expect the big event. At 4 p.m. I was on the phone talking to a friend when I began to feel quite weird — shaky, and my stomach was upset. Slightly nauseated, I also had to go to the bathroom. I began fantasizing that I would be too ill to help with Christmas Eve dinner at my mother's home, that I would simply have to spend the evening lying down. It was probably just something I had eaten, I thought. An hour later, whatever it was had passed, and I left for Mother's feeling great. We had an enjoyable celebration with the family. Later, as I fell asleep about midnight, I was disappointed that nothing I had expected or hoped for had happened.

Awakening the next morning, I realized my second rite of passage had occurred the day before when I felt physically ill. I couldn't believe that I had once again failed to realize, as it was occurring, that what I was experiencing was actually my rite of passage. The symptoms had been much milder than during the winter solstice, but they were almost exactly the same. I hadn't experienced any kind of revelation or visitation from my spirit guides as I had imagined. I did feel extremely energized and also balanced, grounded, and at peace. A couple of days later, however, back in Tallahassee, I began to feel extremely tired, and my eyes felt constantly irritated.

I dreamed that my car engine burst into flames. Many people kept bringing water, but it continued to burn. Through Joshua I was told that my rites of passage were the times when the energy from my initiation was actually brought into my body on the physical level. This had caused a cleansing and a release of toxins which would last for about two weeks. Obviously, my body (or car in the dream) needed a lot of water as it went through this cleansing (or fire in the dream). I was to eat certain foods and drink certain juices, exercise briskly, take B vitamins and do specific yoga exercises to facilitate this cleansing. I was also to have a chiropractic adjustment and refrain from having sex. Within two weeks, the sluggishness was gone, and my eyes returned to normal. Again, as after the Harmonic Convergence, many people commented on how much younger I looked. Another result of both the initiation and the Harmonic Convergence was what seemed to be an almost inexhaustible source of energy once my body had adjusted to the physical changes. I went to bed at night not because I was tired, but because I thought I should.

Not long after my initiation, Lama Sing spoke in a Voyager Project reading about different levels of consciousness. I submitted a question concerning the two consciousness level changes, or vibratory level changes, I had experienced. I wondered if a vibratory level change was a common occurrence and if I would experience a similar change again during this lifetime. He answered: "The transition through vibratory levels is not always noted consciously by entities in the Earth. Those who are seeking and have strived to attune themselves may more probably note such transitions. And they are just that — transitional times in the Earth where, for all intents and purposes, you are passing through a sort of microcosmic experience likened unto that called death. You are leaving behind, collectively, an array of old habits, attitudes, and intents and purposes and adopting simultaneously new ones. These are times of jubilance for the guides and for those whom are in service with you. The population in general might not note this, but they would note some difference, and most of them would do so in retrospect. See?

"You will, we are almost certain, experience this again during this lifetime, and you will experience it when you depart — very similar but much more wondrously, you know, with all the accompanying sounds, lights, and experiences, much more vividly than you can imagine. Something to be looked upon with joyous anticipation, even though the prospect of what you call death in the Earth is not generally thought of in that sense or term.

"More straightforwardly, to state what this is, it is a change in the spiritual level of acceptance while yet in physical body. It is an objective to be sought after and is highly desired. Very often those who work with manipulation, massage, chiropractic, physicians, medical practitioners, those who work in a professional sense with the development of the intuitive abilities — all of these might feel these, note these more significantly than those who do not find themselves involved in such."

I look forward to passing once again into a new energy here on Mother Earth. And I especially look forward to my departure from Mother Earth, when I will awaken and find that I am home.

Chapter 12

# Healing My Heart

$\mathcal{E}$ ach winter the Omega Institute of Rhinebeck, New York, holds wonderful workshops at Maho Bay on St. John, Virgin Islands. Attending for the first time in January of 1991, I met several wonderful teachers including Pat Rodegast, who channels a spirit known as Emmanuel.

As long as I can remember, I have always suffered from the fear of speaking in a group. Heart pounding, palms sweating, face and chest flushing a bright red, and voice shaking, I suffer tremendously when called upon to speak.

During a gathering in which Pat was channeling Emmanuel, he answered my question about this fear with the following comments: "When one has been taught to listen very carefully to see where the danger is coming from — when one has been taught at an early age that one is constantly open to criticism, that there are standards that a small child knows that she cannot fulfill — then it is no wonder, is it, that you wish to hide. For it seems as though there is a guarantee of failure, of mockery, of humiliation, of despair if one has to be seen, to be present as you are, truly are in the moment. For there is a nobility in you that does not want to misrepresent who you are. Have you any idea how wondrous that is, how courageous, and how filled with integrity you really are? And so it is the mind that weaves the webs of illusion, that says to you, you're not who you're supposed to be because you're not who they expect you to be.

"And so, if you begin to speak, you are either going to have to perform and belie the truth of who you are, or you had better just sit down where it is safe and remain quiet. A voice of truth such as your own is one of the rarest gifts to enter into the human world. You all have voices of truth — some of them more buried than others. When you bring yourselves from the world of spirit, that's what you do. You bring your selves from the world of spirit. You are the gift. And though you are all taught, and you (Robin), most certainly in childhood, to fulfill expectation in order to be safe, the truth of it is, there is no other master but your own heart.

"How does one move beyond the fear of speaking

in public? Why, see everyone in public as who you are
— beings of light, sitting inside physical bodies, hoping
somebody is going to say something of truth so then
they can move from your courage. The illusion of
differentness is the illusion of loneliness, is the illusion
of danger. I will say more to you at another time if I
might....

"When you are moved to speak, allow it. And if fear
says that you are going to be afraid, let that not matter.
Fear is something you have cloaked yourself with. It is
not new, it is not new to any of you; don't give it any
kind of majesty. It is just familiar illusion, that's all.
Connect with what your heart wants to say, and then
stand up and shout. You have no idea what a blessing
you will be for so many other people when you decide
to do that."

I continue to struggle with this fear. As promised,
Emmanuel had more to say to me during that trip. I was
told to become unburdened, beginning with releasing
the enormous wit with which I had been taught to deal
most unkindly with myself. Emmanuel assured us that
self-punishment is not ennobling, that we don't need
punishment and never have. Regardless of how difficult
they may become, no child requires punishment nor
deserves it. Punishment, self-judgment, self-cruelty could
no longer be allowed in my life, and should not be allowed in anyone's life.

The last day of the workshop, I took part in an incredibly powerful guided meditation led by Michael Lee,
a yoga teacher. Meditating while lying on a mound of
sand on the beach to open the heart chakra, I began my

journey to heal my heart. I saw a couple of flashes of light that let me know that my guides were with me, and then:

*The healer within comes onto the shore in a bubble of light. I look down at the healer's (my) feet. They are strong and healthy and straight. I am standing at a door which is very thick, rich and deep in color. I open the door and step inside to meet something or someone I am going to heal. I find a very vulnerable child/woman there — every part of myself that has ever been hurt and doesn't feel, doesn't know the beauty inside. To heal her, I embrace her fully, and all those parts disappear into the strong, whole healer. The child/woman becomes complete and whole and totally healed.*

*I see one of my guides — a male with long hair and piercingly beautiful eyes — who tells me that this is part of my initiation, that now I can step forth in my full power totally healed.*

*As I prepare to return to the door, there is a crystal ball on the ground. I pick it up. It is radiating light, and I am told this represents the light within me that will reflect out, touching all that I meet. I place the crystal ball between my heart and solar plexus. I am told that it is an eternal light, always shining within, that I can always call upon and will always be there to light the way and reflect the light and love within outwardly to the world.*

As my consciousness returned to the beach, I was deeply moved. Crying, I thanked my guides for their love and the Creator for my life and His infinite love.

Chapter 13

# Meeting Mathias

*L* ife went on, with all the challenges of being a divorced mother of three and working as a massage therapist. I continued to do readings for friends and acquaintances through the automatic writing. My dream journals were filled as night after night, I had vivid and prophetic dreams. I had learned from Lama Sing during a project on crystals that an amethyst cluster, placed under one's bed in approximate alignment with the solar plexus chakra, stimulates dreaming. It certainly had that effect for me personally. In fact, I sometimes wished I would have a break from remembering my dreams night after night.

In the Spring of 1991 during a reading with Joshua, I was introduced to a new spirit guide named Mathias. I was told that together we had done healing works with crystals in Atlantis and that during a lifetime as Essenes, Mathias had been a mentor of mine who taught me how to use certain energies in the body for healing. He was now present to aid, support, encourage, and advise me on certain decisions ahead that were important because they would help to more perfectly align me with my spiritual purpose and ideal during this lifetime. When I felt the familiar stirring within my heart or when I meditated, I was to call upon him, quiet my mind, and then I was simply to listen.

Mathias had these words for me: "The Earth is entering into a time of purging so it can be healed of those influences which limit, which do not support, those who truly in their hearts seek to be a part of the light and of the works of the Master himself. Do not think of these times which are ahead as being those which will imply loss, but rather there will potentially be gain on all levels for you. As you strive, and as you have taken action to support the light and to be a contribution to it, you have made known your willingness to be used in those works which are necessarily going to be needed for those who will moreso recognize the state of spiritual, mental, emotional, and physical disease in which they have been living, or dwelling.

"You have heard in the past that before the physician can heal, the physician must be healed him or herself. This is not to imply that you are in a state of disease. Rather, the influences which are intended to be a part of the activities ahead for you are those which are going to be moreso involved with getting it all in order — smoothing out the edges."

He wanted me to know that he would be with me, supporting and encouraging me, and that he was coming forward in the name of the Christ, for he knew that I loved the Master as he did. Mathias sent me his blessings and his love and his good wishes and his prayers — not only his prayers, but the prayers of all those who had joined together with him. He had come forth to assist me in my spiritual growth and development. I was also told that if I wanted to do automatic writing with him, he was present and available for that as well.

Once again, I was overwhelmed by the love which I was receiving. Spending time alone, as I often did, on a tiny island a couple of hours away from home, I allowed my gratitude and love for the Creator to fill me and heal me.

### "On Loving God"

Peace descends upon me
And I am free
As I feel you
Walking here with me.

My love bursts free
And takes flight
With the bird flying over me.

Ever present Your love
In each grain of sand

And sound of the sea;
Once again you take my hand.

And fill my heart
With joy so sweet,
With wondrous love of which I'm part.

Soon after meeting Mathias, I took a trip to Jamaica
with a friend. I decided to try some automatic writing
with my new friend in spirit. I had never called on a
specific guide before for the readings, but always the
Higher Self of the person receiving the reading. The first
communication I received from Mathias through automatic writing was as follows: "Reserve the right to just
lie back and relax (I suppose he was speaking about that
part of me that was not frantically writing), releasing all
tensions and fears. For what lies ahead is an experiment,
an experience in channeling — being a channel of light,
of love, and of joy.

"We come to you because in past you have been
available for us — available for us in your wisdom, your
love. Choose freedom — the freedom to allow yourself
the full power of your love, your openness, your willingness to be a channel, a channel working for and of
the light. For many will benefit as a result of your openness, your willingness to be as a light in the darkness.
This darkness is man's separation from his true spirit, his
true oneness with God.

"It is all a matter of acceptance, faith, and joy. Joy is
our true nature. The opportunities are boundless —
boundless if one only has faith in God and in himself.

For within lies all love, all light, which is needed for all things. We are truly unlimited. Each soul accepts exactly what it is ready to accept in its spiritual growth and development.

"You have opened yourself to a great degree in the recent past, opened up to your potential; and now you are experiencing the joy that has resulted — the incredible, indescribable beauty and joy that come from true faith and love of God. You are to demonstrate these things to others, to be as a light. You will help to open many hearts, to shed much light upon the dark recesses of their hearts and minds. Thank you for your willingness to be used in this work. For the more workers, the greater and more swiftly comes the light, moving the Earth's consciousness ahead into what it is meant to be — one of joy, love, sharing, growth, and much potential.

"The Earth will evolve into a much healthier, more beautiful existence. Pain, fear, and guilt will be overcome with the help of those willing to serve as a beacon, to guide others through the darkness onto the one true path, the path of love.

"Through your meditation, we will guide you, be with you always to assist in whatever way we can. Have faith in yourself and your abilities; for you are capable of unlimited power, unlimited joy, and unveiling to many numbers great truth. We love you and are honored to be here with you in this work. Accept our presence and our assistance in joy; for you are very deserving of all the good that comes to you.

(Writing through my tears, I heard:) "The heart is filled with love in this moment; your eyes are filled with tears as you feel the tremendous outpouring of love and joy that is in this work. Radiate this incredible love and joy to others. You are an example of what life can be — fulfilling in every aspect. We release you now and thank you for this opportunity to come forward. Shalom."

I had heard the word "shalom" before but didn't know what it meant. It was certainly not a word I would have chosen, which helped me to believe that I hadn't just fabricated this message. It was sometimes still difficult to believe and accept the tremendous love and support I was receiving.

I continued to meet regularly with Mathias that spring and channel his words. Before long, I was encouraged to choose the subject of the information myself. I chose a number of general topics such as patience and forgiveness. I have self-published a collection of these writings entitled *Messages from Mathias*.

Chapter 14

# Mother Mary

*J* ust a month after meeting Mathias, I journeyed to
Italy for a two-week gathering with Brant. I hadn't
been able to sleep well for several days, perhaps because
of the excitement, and so I began the trip quite exhausted. Looking out the window of the plane, I saw
the shadow of the plane in the clouds encircled by a
beautiful rainbow. I took it as an auspicious omen for
the trip. As a young college student, I had studied in
Florence for six months, had loved Italy, and was looking forward to returning.

There were a dozen or so Germans and three other
Americans attending the workshop. One of the Ger-

man men I had met at Mt. Rainier told me that I looked much younger, almost like a totally different person, than I had at that gathering. I felt like I was a different person, so much had happened in the nine months since then.

A few days later, the same man told me that he would knock on my door when he was ready to go into town so that I could have a ride with him. Later, I left my room and discovered that he had left me behind. I was extremely upset by this. Crying uncontrollably, I didn't know why I was overreacting to being left behind. The tears seemed to flow from a bottomless well of sadness. I cried off and on all day.

Confused, I decided to meditate and ask my guides why I was overreacting. I was told that in another lifetime I had been an Estruscan, and my mother had died when I was very young. I was raised by an old man and looked after by many in the village. Though I didn't actually have any memory of that lifetime, the emotional memory of abandonment, which had been triggered by being left behind, was very real. I cried for days, releasing the pain and suffering I had felt during that incarnation. Until that emotional cleansing, every time my children would leave to visit their father, I would feel extremely abandoned and depressed. After returning from Italy, I discovered that that reaction had disappeared completely.

One day during the seminar, our group visited the church of St. Francis of Assisi. Just before leaving for Italy, a psychic had told me that I would find something spiritual during the journey, and she saw a dove around it. Her prediction was to come true, and I couldn't in my wildest imaginings have guessed the events which I now relate.

The church outside of Assisi is very simple, but the energies of love and peace that are present both inside the church and outside on the grounds are so strong that they are almost overwhelming. I walked along a path outside, passing a huge wooden cross. At the end of the path there was an altar, and on the wall at the back of the altar was a painting of the Virgin Mary and baby Jesus. They had very beautiful, very golden halos. Alone, I stood entranced by the beauty of the painting.

I clearly heard the Virgin say, "Thee art a friend of ours."

I immediately answered out loud, "Yes, I am."

Then I stood there in shock, wondering if what I thought had just happened had truly happened. I started walking back towards the church, and I heard the sound of wings flapping.

A young boy looked at me and asked excitedly, "Did you see the doves?"

Smiling, I answered, "No, but I heard them."

Chapter 15

## Vision Quest

*A* few days before leaving Italy, Brant prepared us for a vision quest by holding an all night ceremony. It was quite cold. We sang, prayed, and danced all night. We had no food and were allowed our last drink of water around 4 a.m. Exhausted by the emotions of the previous events, I kept slumping and nodding off.

At sunrise most of us left the circle, climbing up a nearby mountain with our gear. The climb was quite difficult for me, as tired as I was. When I felt I could walk no longer, I found a beautiful spot under a pine tree. I placed stones in each of the four directions, one in the center for my heart, and stones as well for the lower, middle, and upper worlds. This was to be my circle of light, my protection during the vision quest. Praying, I planted the prayer arrow I had made.

I fell asleep quickly, and in a dream I saw three circles touching each other in a row, each one with an inverted triangle within it. I was told later through Joshua that the circles represented infinity, or the Creator, and the triangles, man in the Earth — thus man in the Earth merged with the Creator. My ideals and consciousness, according to my guides, had reached a point where I was potentially capable of accepting myself as being at one with God. This was news to me.

I woke up, remembered the dream, and then went back to sleep. The next time I woke up, a small fire had started in the grass from a candle I had lit. Dazed from a lack of sleep, I had forgotten to put the candle out after planting my prayer arrow. I put the fire out with my hands and a rattle. Stepping outside of the circle only to go to the bathroom, I spent the day sitting or lying down, looking at a lake in the distance, the woods, the grass and trees, the sky, and the birds and insects. I felt the energy of these and all living things.

At sunset, I was looking at the beautiful pink sky and noticed a single cloud. I then noticed that it looked like the profile of a face. Then I saw that it was Don Jose, Brant's teacher, who was smiling and laughing. I had never met Don Jose, but recognized him from the slides Brant had shown us.

Falling asleep as soon as it got dark, I slept fitfully

and awoke just before sunrise. After singing and praying, I hiked down the mountain and returned to the fire which Brant and those remaining behind had kept burning all night as they prayed for our protection. No one could drink until everyone had returned. Brant then led us in ceremony as each of us gave thanks for our vision quest and safe return to the Creator, Grandmother Growth, Mother Earth, and the four directions. We then drank the sacred water. As we sat in the circle after the ceremony, Brant told us that he had had a vision of Don Jose in the sky the night before, just at sunset. He had seen Don Jose's face in the clouds.

In spite of all the wondrous things I had experienced in Italy, there was a part of me that looked forward to going home to Florida. And yet there was another part that did not want to leave this land — that part of me that had called Italy home.

Chapter 16

# The Traveling Show

*I* am watching a large group of people trying out on a stage for a variety of different jobs with a traveling show. *I wonder if there is anything I can do with the show. Then I remember that I am a massage therapist. There is a man sitting in the audience watching the try-outs who is in charge of hiring. I approach him.*

*"Could you use someone who does massage?" I ask.*

*"Yes," he answers.*

*I don't know if I should go with the group, because I don't know what I'll do with my daughters. When I tell the man this, he tells me to let him know what I decide.*

*I speak to my daughters. My ten-year-old tells me she wants to come. There are a lot of kids in the group. I am worried about what to do with my older daughter if she doesn't want to come. She finally speaks to some people in the group and decides to come too. I ask the man where we are going.*

*"We are going to a very small town called Midland, near the West Coast," he tells me.*

*I am a bit concerned about how I am going to get paid, because I don't know exactly what I'll be doing. It seems I'll be doing a lot of things. I don't want to receive a salary for my massage work. I tell the man in charge I get $40 an hour for massage.*

The scene switches.

*The girls and I go with a woman to a beautiful spring in Crystal River, Florida. We swim in the spring.*

*The woman asks, "Isn't this beautiful?"*

*I have tears in my eyes as I answer, "Yes, I practically grew up here. I know it well, and it holds a lot of memories for me. My family has been coming here for many years."*

My family did, in fact, have a second home in Crystal River, and I had many wonderful memories of time spent there. I would surely miss that beautiful river if I moved to Midland, wherever the hell that was. Thus began a series of dreams about moving that began soon after my return from Italy and continued throughout the summer. As both Lama Sing and Merlin had foretold, everything in my life was about to change, and moving would certainly make "one day separated from the other seem like two different lifetimes," as Lama Sing had said. I had learned to trust my dreams. In the past when I had followed my guiding dreams, all had been well. The few times I had ignored obvious messages received during sleep, I had had negative experiences as a result.

So now my job was to discover exactly where Midland was. The only Midland I had ever heard of was in Texas, which obviously wasn't near the West Coast. So I got out my encyclopedias. I first scanned the list of all the towns and cities in California - no Midland. I decided to try Oregon next. There it was, eight miles south of a town called Klamath Falls. There was no population listed for Midland — well, that certainly qualified it as a small town! Just out of curiosity, I checked to see if there was a Midland in Washington; there wasn't.

Calling the Chamber of Commerce in Klamath Falls, I told the man who answered I was considering moving to Midland, and I asked how many people lived there.

Laughing, he said "Oh, about fifty."

I had always heard how beautiful Oregon is. Quite excited by the prospect of living there, I imagined Midland to be very green and lush, with trees everywhere.

But then I realized that my son had not been present in the dream. He had one year to finish before graduating from high school. Considering the possibility that he may not want to move across the country with us filled me with great sadness. There was going to be nothing easy about leaving everyone and everything I knew, but leaving my son behind would be even more difficult.

I began having trouble sleeping. One of my eyes was red and painful. I had pain in my neck and felt slightly nauseated. Change, even the prospect of change, is not easy.

In my next moving dream, the girls and I were staying in a hotel. We were to move the next day. We changed rooms and were given a room on the ground floor. I thought this was good since it would be easier to leave from the ground floor. The next day when we were leaving, someone had given me a special phone number to call for Delta Airlines. A number of people came over, took our luggage and gave us a ride to the terminal. Everything was taken care of for us. We were the only ones in the terminal. I wondered if this special treatment cost a lot more.

The meaning of this dream wasn't completely clear to me at the time, but I was encouraged by it, as it appeared I would have a lot of help and support. The messages I was receiving from Mathias during the automatic writing at this time were also loving and encouraging. It was like having your dearest friend holding your hand as you step into the unknown. In spite of these beautiful invisible friends, I felt very much alone on the physical plane. I longed for a friend and lover I could touch.

Mathias assured me that the question of a relationship would be resolved soon. I had fantasized about a relationship with a German man I had been attracted to in Italy. I met him in my dreams and thought about him constantly. We wrote to each other, and I hoped he would visit me soon. In one of the messages, Mathias told me that he was the man who was to be my partner — that we would "grow together, work together, laugh together, love together." I wondered if I had put the words in

Mathias's mouth, so to speak, because I wanted a relationship so much. I knew time would tell.

Around this time I developed a cyst in the eyelid of my right eye which was really sore and bothersome. I tried all kinds of remedies; it would get smaller for a while, then grow larger again. I was told through Joshua that it was present to help me know the degree to which I was allowing my spiritual sight to become obscured. I wondered if my romantic fantasies were just an illusion because of my desire to find my soulmate. Was this the reason I had this big lump in my eyelid? And if it was an illusion, could I ever trust my messages from Mathias again? Did Mathias really exist, or did I just put his name to those things I wanted to hear? Was I really going to move all the way across the country to a town I had never seen and where I knew no one?

My dreams continued to foretell events surrounding my move. In one, I managed to escape from somewhere I'd been held captive. My ex-husband and son were left behind, unable to escape. Less than a week later, I dreamed that I was told that some people were going to move. There was a sheet of paper with the names of those who were going to move circled. There were three of them. Obviously, my son would be staying behind with his father.

*The girls and I are in Oregon. My older daughter and I are outside, and the weather is beautiful — just like springtime in Tallahassee. I say to her, "See, honey, every day is spring here."*

*"Yes," she answers.*

This was a beautiful and encouraging dream, but in

reality I continued to suffer physically from the stress of preparing for the changes ahead. My eye was infected, I had constant back pain, and I was frequently depressed. I knew where I was moving, but not when. I assumed that since I had been told where I would live, that eventually I would also be told when. I began to clean closets and pack some boxes in preparation.

One day when I was feeling particularly stressed out, Mathias began "knocking" at my heart rather insistently. I intuitively felt he wanted to communicate with me, so I sat down, pen in hand, to receive his message. He encouraged me to have faith and to be patient. My eye would heal, and part of the discomfort I was experiencing was some cleansing in preparation for the move. I was encouraged to meditate as often as possible, for my guides had the ability, with my permission, to assist me during meditation in returning to a place of balance and ease. I was told that a mental attitude of joy, faith in the perfection of the events that were transpiring, and an attitude of peace and calmness would aid my transition and all the preparation that would go into it. Virtually everything in my life would be different, but there would be an increase in joy, in purpose, and in love. He closed his message with, "We love you and thank you for heeding our 'knocking' at the door of your heart."

I was still perplexed as to exactly when I would move. Then one of my friends reminded me of a dream I had had a couple of months earlier about an appointment with my chiropractor for an adjustment. In that dream, I had to wait for a friend to return from his appointment, and then it was extremely important that I leave

almost immediately upon his return for my appointment at exactly 9:30. Suggesting that this dream was
guidance as to when I should make a trip to Midland to
prepare for my move, she suggested I was to fly to Klamath Falls on September 30th, or 9/30. As soon as the
words were out of her mouth, I felt she was right. After
all, moving across the country was going to be a major
adjustment, but I didn't need a chiropractor for this one.

I decided to take my younger daughter with me to
check out Midland. We planned to rent a car at the
airport, drive the few minutes to Midland, and look
around once we got there. If we happened to see a house
for sale that looked interesting, we would make an appointment to see it. I had faith that I would be guided
each step of the way. I was not to be disappointed.
Deciding that five days would be enough to fulfill our
mission to find our new home, I made the plane reser-
vations.

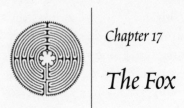

Chapter 17

## The Fox

*M*y faith was tested and badly shaken when one of my best friends returned from a visit with a psychic and told me that the woman, in the middle of her reading, had given her a message for me: I should not move, the man I was interested in was a gigolo, and the cyst in my eyelid would have to be lanced. I felt sure of nothing anymore.

While at home one evening at sunset, I heard an almost unearthly cry of a wild animal. I had never heard such a sound before, but instinctively knew what it was. Looking out the front door, I saw a beautiful red fox standing in my driveway staring right at me, through me. I stared back. The fox, like the owl I had seen on Mount Haleakala, seemed so surreal. I realized I was experiencing another visitation from spirit. After a time, the fox slipped away.

I wondered what significance seeing the fox had. A cousin had recently given me a set of Medicine Cards. Similar to Tarot Cards, they can be used for divination. Unlike Tarot Cards, each card represents a different animal spirit. I had never used them for divination, but especially enjoyed reading the accompanying book, which spoke about animal medicine and each of the creatures represented by the cards. Each animal of the Medicine Cards represents a particular lesson in life through which understanding and healing can occur. It is a beautiful book which teaches us that all humans have much to learn from the animal kingdom. The teachings found in the book are handed down from many native traditions.

Looking up the fox, I learned that this animal protects the family, is adaptable, observant, and swift in thought and action. The fox is quickly decisive and sure-footed in the physical world. Representing good luck for those traveling afar, I felt it was a good omen for our move. Fox medicine taught me that I would do well to observe others silently. I could learn much from the actions of others rather than their words. I decided that rather than place any value in the words of that psychic, I would rely upon my own instincts and inner knowledge as the events in my life unfolded.

Awakening at dawn the next morning, I walked

downstairs to make some tea. I saw the fox outside once again. As he slowly circled the entire house, I moved with him, going from room to room, inside the house. When he had completed the circle, he left. I thanked him for his visitation and teachings.

I was about to complete another circle of sorts. I was planning to return to a workshop with Brant at Feathered Pipe. In the year since I had first met Brant there, I had traveled in the four directions to join his gatherings — first north and west to Montana, then further west to Mt. Rainier, south to Mexico, and east to Italy.

As I prepared to return to Montana, my nervous system was taxed almost to its limit. One day in yoga class, my teacher spent about thirty minutes practicing pranayama, the yogic breathing exercises. I had felt the benefits of these exercises before, but this time I felt a total shift in my energy and in my nervous system. For the first time, I truly understood what an effective tool breathing can be. Those thirty minutes took me from the edge of a nervous breakdown to a state of peace and relaxation. Another great help I discovered was "Amino Relaxer," an amino acid supplement which acted as a safe and effective alternative to allopathic tranquilizers.

I once again felt strong in my faith and purpose. I decided to release my concern about finding that special relationship in my life. I remembered Lama Sing telling me that each one of us is already complete and that the purpose of life might well be stated as a quest for discovery of that completeness. Upon my arrival at

## The Fox

Feathered Pipe, I discovered that my German friend wasn't present for the gathering, as I'd hoped. I did not allow myself to be disappointed. I decided to let go and let God.

Chapter 18

# Message from the Master

*T*he summer of 1991 was drawing to a close. In September, my daughter and I would go to Midland. Joshua was in town, and at the end of a reading with him, the energy in the room changed. There seemed to be more light in the room, and I saw an aura of white light around Joshua. He told me that the Master was present and had the following message for me: "He wants me to tell you that in the spiritual sense, He is placing His hands on your forehead to give you His personal blessing for your willingness to be faithful and your persistent and dedicated and pure-hearted desire to be used in God's service. He says that you are joining an army of individuals who are, like yourself, already awakened but being awakened in the Earth, who will help to bring in a new age of enlightenment and spiritual alignment into the Earth.

"He wants to recognize you and tell you that you and others have been in the front lines in the sense that you've been meeting the tests and the challenges and the potential obstacles first; that you have met these with dignity and with, as best you were able to muster at the time, good humor.

"He is with you, and He is here to counsel and to guide you. He'll be at your side to lend whatever support and encouragement is necessary for you to do what's ahead. Don't worry about tomorrow, but take care of what is happening today."

I was filled with love and wonder that I would be so honored. Energetically, after that reading, I felt quite different — very centered and balanced, very confident.

I continued to have dreams which related to the move. In one of them, I was cleaning up a house that was a mess, but it had been clean to start with, so I knew there was hope for it. I interpreted this to mean that the house I would find in Midland would need some cleaning and fixing up. In another dream, I was part of a wedding party. Was marriage to be part of my new life in Midland? The German man and I continued to write to each other. I tried not to fantasize about our relationship, but had only partial success.

The fox paid me another visit one afternoon. I was outside and saw him moving through the yard. As I noticed him, he stopped, turned, and stared at me. I thought perhaps he was present to wish me well on a trip to Mexico I was taking in a few days to a Huichol village with Brant and a small group.

About a week after that trip, my daughter and I left for Midland. My dream about an adjustment had been prophetic. In that dream, a friend had returned from an appointment, and then I left almost immediately for my appointment, which was exactly at 9:30. I was obviously the "friend." I left for Midland on September 30th, or 9/30, less than a week after my return from Mexico.

On the plane, my daughter shared what she had written in her journal — that she felt God was giving her a chance to start over with this move. My heart was filled with a mother's love for her sweetness and her courage and willingness to venture into the unknown as I dragged her across the country to follow my dream. I had faith that God was guiding our steps.

*Faith is an essence or a quality which is almost without definition, because the very attempt to define same limits it; and faith, by its nature, has no limit. Faith is a quality which is knowing. Faith is an essence of God, which is Godly. Faith is a quality of life which, when lived, is utterly liberating. Fear is vanquished by the presence of faith. And faith, in and of itself, is a spiritual quality which is one of the most powerfully accelerating for an individual. Faith enables an entity to transit untold and unknown realms of expression. Faith is the cloak of God's joy surrounding his*

*children. It is, when claimed, impenetrable. Faith can be given and shared in a manner which is remarkable to behold and to experience. Faith can be given from one to another just in the manner that you would scoop up a handful of grains of sand at the seashore and hand that to another. Literally. Faith is contagious. It is extremely powerful in the continuum of energies. See?*
~ *Lama Sing*

Chapter 19

*Midland*

*W*hen I stepped off the plane in Klamath Falls, I wondered where the lush, green Oregon I was expecting was. Where were the trees? Everything was so brown. I tried to see the beauty in the stark brown mountains, but it was difficult. I had had no idea I would be living in the high desert. Trying to hide my disappointment from my daughter, I rented a car and got directions to Midland.

As we drove, I didn't see anything that would have consciously attracted me to the area. We found the one store and tiny post office in the town. It appeared the only restaurant, which was next door, was closed. It seemed to be a rather economically depressed area of mostly small farms. I wondered why I was here. I had faith that I was in the right place, but after seeing it, I certainly wouldn't have chosen it myself. And yet, at the same time, I also knew that I *had* chosen it. Between lifetimes, our spirits choose events, conditions, and opportunities our earthly personalities may not ever desire, but which our spirits have determined are necessary or conducive to our spiritual growth.

As we drove around the area, my daughter spotted a house alone on a hill and said, "That's our house."

I said, "I'll believe that if there's a 'for sale' sign in front of it."

Approaching the house, we saw that it was indeed for sale. After calling the real estate agent from a phone booth, we met her at the house shortly. We decided it wasn't our house — there were just too many repairs to be made.

The agent told us, "There's a home going on the market tomorrow that I think you may like." We made plans to look at that house the next day. The owners had just decided to put it on the market.

Settled in a motel room in Klamath Falls, I checked the yellow pages to see what was available in the city. There was only one health food store, and yoga wasn't even listed! It seemed that the community didn't offer the things that I enjoyed and had grown used to.

The next day before meeting the realtor, I prayed for guidance in finding our new home. I was encouraged and comforted by Mathias's presence, which I was made aware of by the familiar activity in my heart.

We went to see the house with the realtor. It was on the side of a hill and had an incredibly beautiful view of Mt. Shasta, a majestic mountain which was just over the border in California. As in my dream, it was a bit of a mess, but nothing that some cleaning and remodeling wouldn't fix. My daughter and I knew, without a doubt, that this was the home we had come to find. If we had come a week earlier, it wouldn't have been for sale yet, and a week later perhaps already sold. Two days after our arrival, the owners had accepted my offer, and we were to move into it just a month later.

Our remaining three days were spent exploring the area. Mt. Shasta captured our hearts with its unspoiled beauty and power and majesty; and Crater Lake, a deep blue lake in the crater of an inactive volcano, was truly a wonder to behold. We realized that our new land offered much beauty to discover and enjoy. Returning from Crater Lake, a red fox crossed the road right in front of our car.

*And this is good for all. If you are seeking to make a change, whether it's a major change or a minimal change by your measure, remember that so doing can bring about a state of joy or a condition of anxiety, questions, doubts, uncertainty. One of the ways to make such a transition even, balanced, joyful and at ease is to utterly release the past, giving thanks for having had the experience or experiences — blessing those, in all respects, whom have supported, encouraged, sheltered and nourished*

*you, referring to all of the expressions of God's
energies that would include your former residence,
your associates, your friends and so forth, and also
turning to look forward to the future and inviting,
with the same attitude of blessing and cheer,
whatever works and experiences God knoweth to
be the highest and best for you.*
~ Lama Sing

Chapter 20

## *Moving On*

*J* ust a few days after our return to Florida from Midland, I had a phone reading with Diana. Before she began, she told me that she saw a wolf baying at the moon. Then Merlin came forward with the following message: "Good day and blessings to you, dear one. It is I, one who is termed the madcap Merlin. The mischievous and mysterious Merlin, and we would ask who might you be, dear one? This is more than Robin who speaks, hmmm? This is many who speak.

"Now. What I would like you to comprehend at this time is that you are perhaps to be known as "Robin of

Many Tongues," because there are many who are going to speak through you. It is your destiny to be in alignment with the higher truth, and it is your destiny to be as a mouthpiece, as it were, for those higher truths. You will find that when you make this move, that there will be a shift or an alignment that occurs within you that allows your gifts to come forward in a much more profound and a much more powerful way. You are to begin to speak as a channel speaks — to allow yourself not only to try this which is termed the automatic writing, but to sit down, perhaps with a friend or with a tape recorder or with a friend and a tape recorder, so to speak, and to allow that which comes in the name of the Christ to speak through you.

"Now. You have undergone many internal adjustments in order for this to occur, and the location that you are traveling to is, what one might term, a spiritual vortex, a place where ideas can enter in and exit in a much greater ease than where you are now. It is also true that you are leaving behind the old Robin or the limited Robin or the one who only perceived herself as a single unit. As you make this travel across the country, you are also coming back to a place of, what we will term, your roots — a time when you have been in body previously as a medicine woman, a time where you were quite a profound seer and quite a profound healer. So one of the things that this area holds for you is memory.

"In any time frame in any place in the world or, in truth, in any place in the universe, when a being makes an offering to that place, that offering remains in the consciousness of that place. What is there for you, then, is a template of past accomplishments, a template that will be reabsorbed into your being that will help activate you at a greater speed and a template which will accelerate you into alignment with your specific timeline for this lifetime. Then, since you were and are just a bit behind where you should be, if it feels as if things are moving quite fast, it is true because you are being accelerated to a specific alignment upon your own spiritual timeline which will allow you to be more present with your gifts and with your abilities.

"Now. What you have separated from in the past is like shedding a skin, and you will never be the same. This new skin that you are wearing is the skin of a medicine woman. It is the skin of, what I'm going to term, a certain root race that was here among the beginnings of time upon this planet. Are you familiar with this book which is termed *The Bird Tribe*? This is the book that you should read. It is the book about how highly evolved souls came in to various tribes on this North American continent, and how it is that they intermingled with the peoples that were here.

"You will begin to have memory when you arrive in this place of your new location. You will begin to have memory of being there before and of having done ceremony there before and of having led ceremony there before. You will also have memory of what occurred when the white man came. You must come to a point of seeing yourself in both shoes, both as the medicine person and as the white man. See yourself as a reflection of the whole — of both sides of the coin, of the light and the dark, of the truth and the untruth — and just begin to allow the land to speak to you again.

"Now. When you make this transition, there is going to be a lot that comes up in you almost immediately. It will be almost as if you are being, in some way, sacrificed. In another form, we would term it initiation. In another form, it is like losing one skin after another. Think about how long it took you to shed this last skin. You are aware of that. It was kind of a painful and drawn out process, hmmm? And now you have this new skin on, and you feel better; but the new skin is also temporary, and what you are going to pass through, then, in this new place, is a series of initiations and a series of new skins. The reason is that you are being accelerated. So what is going to happen here is you are going to need to understand at the personality level that there won't be anything that is termed structure, and there won't be anything which is termed security or safety, so to speak; and it is not so much that these things are going to affect your outside world but the inner world, or perhaps feel as if everything is breaking up, so to speak.

"Now. This does not mean that there will not be some stability in the home, in the family and on and on. I am not talking about the outer world breaking up so much as I am talking about the inner world. So it is time for you to let go of all the formulas, hmmm?, all the belief systems; everything that you think you have tucked into your pocket that is right is probably going to go through many, many transformations before it settles into your pocket again.

"Now. The reason that I am telling you this is obvious, hmmm? so that you will not be overwhelmed, and you will not be freaked out, so to speak, and that you will just flow, because the changes are going to be many — rapid and many. You are going to open up at a very accelerated rate. You will have information being fed to you a great deal. You are going to want to speak, also, this information as it comes through you as in a channeling. What you do have to remember is that you are the one responsible for grounding all of it. Just because information comes through you and passes through you as in a channeling, you also are responsible for grounding it so that it doesn't go into the atmosphere in a kind of nonsensical or erroneous fashion. So it is very important for you to practice all of the techniques that you know about grounding and to ask your guidance what you can do to stay stabilized, to stay grounded, to help the information go into the Earth and root itself.

"It is the concept of — you know how some people have marvelous ideas and they never do anything with them, hmmm? It is that same kind of concept. Nothing will ever happen to the information that you give out if it is not grounded, so you have to learn to be very stable in your physical body, to be very deeply connected to the Earth, and to allow this, these new formulas, these new tongues, these new ideas to come forth into being, but in a very grounded and stable form.

"Now. What I am sending to you today is grounded energy. I am speaking in this tone of voice and in this vibrational form; and you, perhaps, might feel as if you are being nailed into the floor energetically. That is, in a sense, what I am doing as I am pulling you down,

down, down, into the Earth — that each time that you listen to this message you will feel this energy, and it will be a balance to what is coming in. Some very highly programmed information, some very high vibrational information, is going to come through you. In order to handle it, you must stay grounded. You must do your grounding practices.

"Now. Once you are out in this new environment and you have moved into a place of feeling settled, then it will be time for you to go exploring, to get out into nature and to find those spots that are holding these templates that I have spoken of from your past existences. You will be led to them; they will call you, so to speak, and there will be several specific areas in the surrounding area where you are that you will want to go and to meditate on a very regular basis. This will further activate these templates within you which will bring you a great deal of knowledge that is stored in your own system.

"Now. The teachings that you have been following and the teacher (Brant) that you have been following are very worthwhile, and it is important to continue to keep that doorway open for some time until such time that you feel comfortable, in a sense, being your own teacher and coming into contact with teachers who are in spirit, such as myself, such as those who are termed the animal spirits. The one whom Diana saw at the beginning of the reading, this wolf baying at the moon, is to be one of your teachers, and he will come from time to time in your meditations and will lead you on specific journeys and show you specific things that will begin to open the doors to some very powerful past memories and some connection with the spirit of the land where you are relocating.

"This is going to be a time of personal empowerment — a time of receiving and receiving and receiving. This is a good lesson for you, for you are not such a good receiver. You are a better giver than receiver. So this is going to be a very big lesson for you on many different levels.

"The outer work that you do, the healing, the massage, the touching, etc., is not going to change that quickly — not as quickly as what you are perceiving on the inside. What is most important for this next time frame is that you give what you can, but don't be, what I am going to term, overly invested in what you can give. Understand that in time you will give a great deal more, but for this next time frame for you to recognize that you are in a cycle of being given to. What you must do is simply avail yourself and be open and make yourself ready to receive. You must go and seek out these three places that will form, what I might term, a triangular formation, and go and sit at them at various times and meditate and receive the energies from the templates. Yes.

"Now. This one termed Wolf. Wolf is a very powerful being. Wolf is the teacher of the clan. Wolf comes to you to share the teachings that are stored in this land where you are going, also to share some history of the land where you are going and also to share some of the future of the land where you are going. This will not be your final place of residence. It is a, perhaps what I might term, a semi-temporary move. You will be there long enough, indeed, to make it worthwhile, but it is not as if you are going to be staying there the rest of your life. This is an interim move to really repattern and to really reactivate energies which are coming into your being. In many cases, this kind of acceleration and activation is a step-by-step process where one will be led to this place and then to this place and then to this place. Yours is basically going to take place in one place, and the removal that would come from actually moving from one place to another is going to come in the form of shedding skins. Do you comprehend what I am saying? Good.

"So. This life is no longer yours. Do you comprehend this also? It is not yours in the sense of you, the personality, having control over it. In a sense, you have given that up quite some time ago in a ceremony. You let go, and now what we term spirit is in the driver's seat. Sometimes the personality doesn't understand what spirit is doing. Sometimes the personality will want to yell at spirit. Sometimes the personality will want to walk away from spirit. Sometimes the personality will want to step on the brakes, but let me say this to you: know that you are more your spirit than your personality, and when the personality begins to fear, or the personality begins to want to change the direction that things are going in, stop for a moment and see how you are invested in the personality's fears and expectations and simply pull your energies back into center and allow the personality to go through whatever it needs to go through and then continue on your way.

"Now. In the beginning of this reading we set up

the vibrations of silence. In the vibrations of silence, there is much which can be transmitted. It is why we are speaking slowly and pausing a great deal. What is being transmitted to you in the spaces and the pauses is actually more powerful and more meaningful than what we are saying. In truth, we could sit here for our time and say nothing, and the messages would be sent to you, and you would receive a deep seating and a very deep healing. So we want you to know that when you relisten to this tape that there is much which is unsaid and unheard, but nonetheless, much that is being transmitted.

"Now I want to call upon the glandular system in your body, in your physical body, that relates to the chakra system. More specifically, I want to call upon the pituitary and that which is termed the thymus, and I want there to be further activation in these areas.

"Now. As we activate you will feel, perhaps, what we might term a new strength coming into your being, and you will find a great deal of groundedness coming into your being. This groundedness is for you to remember at all times. We are going to pause for a few more moments and let this transmission come forward to you.

"Now. What is also going to be coming forward during this next time frame for you to assimilate is more balance between your male and female, between your inner male and your inner female. There is a certain hesitation that you have at this moment concerning male energies, and it is being reflected in your outer life, in your relation to certain males. It is a reflection of what is going on inside in relation to your own inner male.

What I would like you to do at this point is to call an image of that inner male forward and tell me how you perceive this one.

"Now. Are you going to be able to put your hand in the hand of this male energy and allow him to lead you in a certain way? Good. So what is going to come up for you are many trust issues — trusting the male — when to, when not to. There is a great deal of this kind of energy about trusting the male that is going to be involved in your next steps here. Sometimes when this happens, it appears that there are many males in your life whom you can not trust, and it appears as if they're plotting against you, so to speak. Do you comprehend? What you have to do is kind of hold your breath and walk through it, because what is happening is that the belief systems that you have in your subconscious mind are going to be coming to the surface and out-picturing themselves around you. What you have to do is to understand that whatever is out-pictured around you is the illusion, and the truth is inside; and the truth about the male energy is inside, and that is where you go to find your strength, and that is where you go to find your direction, and that is where you go to find your support.

"Part of you, we might say, wishes that there would be a male to lean on, hmmm? Yes, part of you. The other part wouldn't trust him if he did show up, so to speak, hmmm? So what is happening here is that there are many double messages that you are putting out into the universe, so what is going to come back to you from the outer world are many double messages. Now, you can get caught in the drama of this, or you can recognize that somehow you are creating all of it. Look at it this way. Do you believe that in the higher realms there are angels and teachers and guides who direct you, hmmm? And do you believe that in your third dimensional existence that thoughts are things, hmmm? So you have belief in the reality of the superconscious, you have belief in the reality of the conscious, and what I want to explain to you is that you must also have belief in the subconscious. And the subconscious puts out energy in the form of thought and feeling which creates in your outside world, which reflect back to you, which, for the most part, people say, 'I don't understand,' or 'Why is this happening to me,' or in some way they feel that life is not being fair. In truth, those kinds of situations are coming as a direct reflection of what is in the subconscious mind.

"Now. What I want you to begin to see, then, in your life, is that these difficulties or disappointments or betrayals or configurations of experience are all part of your own projection whether you can see them or not. So what you do in those situations is to begin to take responsibility — 'O.K., I co-created this situation with so and so; I co-created this situation with so and so; I co-created this event.' When you begin to allow yourself to speak and to comprehend in those terms, then you will begin to see; the light of day begins to pierce the veils of the unconscious mind, and you begin to see what's really going on inside of you.

"Now. As you brought that male vision forward, you were only comfortable with part of him. The other part of him you didn't trust. So what is coming for you also in this time frame, this next time frame that I speak of, is further alignment with the true male energies. So what you are going to perceive is a lot of untrue male energies which are reflections of what you believe inside — what your little girl, perhaps, believes inside, what you have believed from past lives inside. So you begin to now walk this walk which is a very powerful walk, coming into terms with many, many, many different aspects of who you are.

"You are going to be receiving some very high energies, and imagine that there is a diagram in front of you with three levels, one piled on top of the other. You have the subconscious, the conscious and the superconscious. As the superconscious begins to reveal itself, in order for you to stay in balance, the subconscious also has to reveal itself. So this is how the path works. This is how you walk the line between the light and the dark, and this is how you truly learn about yourself.

"Now. Before you marry again, you will have to become the bride of your own male energies, and this will take some time. But the more you give yourself opportunity with the land, the more the healing will come. The more you allow yourself to be just guided from moment to moment, day to day, the more the healing will come. You are destined to be with another partner. It is down the road somewhat, but it will be very clear to you as the time comes.

"Now. Know that this is in order and know that it will occur when it is time, and in the meantime, just relax. Don't worry yourself about who it is or when it is going to happen or if it is going to happen. Let that go because when the moment is right, it will happen. Do you comprehend? Good.

"Now. We are going to enter into one more deep silence. This last silence contained codes that you will use to activate those three places that you are going to find — three places on the land that you will be drawn to. When you get there, use this silence, and it will be the energy that activates those areas and which will cause them to release back to you the information and the activation that is destined to occur. It is like there's a certain configuration of patterned energy in that silence that you will pass on which will create the opening. Good.

"Now. This next year to a year and a half will be a time of activating your own medicine woman. Invite her in, make a space in the home for her, and you will find that she will give you much in return. This path that fascinates you so much is, in a sense, your own path. Funny, hmmm?, how that works.

"So that is going to be my message for you today, dear one. We are most pleased at all that has happened and how you have learned to appreciate all that has been given to you. For a while there it was difficult to appreciate, perhaps, anything. Now you have come to a place of great appreciation of everything. Yes. You are going to be given much more — much, much more. In grounding it and appreciating it, it will come into the correct alignment within you, and there will be a blessedness and a sacredness which both precedes you and follows you wherever you go. Remember this, and when those things appear in your path which seem to be out of order, look inside. Look for the reflection and ask for guidance. This is a great step you are taking here. Your future calls you — which, in truth, is simply your superconscious being that calls you. So that is where you are going, and this move is the next step in the right direction.

"So. I am going to send to you now some doves of peace that they may surround you as you make this transition, and we send to you much love.

"I seal this now in the Star of David, within the seal of Melchizedek, and ask that it be placed into, what I am going to term, a sacred secrecy, a place of silence. Good.

"So. The message has been delivered and I must now take my leave. Blessings to you, dear one and so be it. Blessings."

After this reading, I wondered no more about the purpose of my move. The reading, in spite of the many wonderful things I was told, left me feeling emotionally a bit depressed. What lay ahead for me seemed so intense, so overwhelming. Physically, I had never felt so grounded, so rooted into Mother Earth. I felt wonderful and quite different than I had before the reading. I remembered the dream in which I moved to the ground floor just before the move and that that was a much easier place from which to leave.

There were so many details to take care of in preparation for the move less than a month later. It was a busy and stressful time. I dreamed that I was having car trouble.

The engine was acting up off and on. This dream reflected the physical problems I was having due to the stress. The cyst on my eyelid had finally disappeared, but all of the children and I were having stomach trouble.

I managed to do a few last readings with Mathias for friends and a couple of readings for myself. As always, the love and support my guides expressed to me through the automatic writing helped me through the most difficult of times. Yoga and meditation were invaluable at that time in assisting me to maintain a sense of balance and well-being.

I felt a great sense of sadness as friends and family came to say good-bye, but also a great sense of excitement. The movers packed up all of our belongings as well as my car, and we flew off to our new life and wherever my dreams were to lead us.

Chapter 21

# The Dark Side

*T*he reality of moving to a place where we were familiar with nothing and no one was difficult for all three of us. We had our share of sad and lonely moments. I busied myself with remodeling the house, and the girls quickly made friends at school.

Just a few days after the move, a friend in Florida told me that a relatively new friend of mine there had just been arrested for child molestation. I also learned that he had been imprisoned before I knew him for a murder which had been an act of passion. I had spent quite a bit of time with him in the months before the move. Shocked and upset by this news, I felt it was difficult to know who to trust anymore, and I no longer had faith in my own judgment. I remembered Merlin's words about the males in my life. And I was experiencing that feeling he had described of my inner world breaking apart. I felt alone and lost.

One night, not long after getting settled into our new home, I dreamed that we were going to move somewhere else. It was going to cost a lot less because we wouldn't be moving far away. I decided to let the moving company do all the packing. Since we weren't going as far this time, it wouldn't be as expensive. The dream confirmed what Merlin had told me about Midland not being my final place of residence. I was pleased that the next move would not be as major as the one I'd just experienced.

One night I had an extremely disturbing dream: *I have a son. He tries to kill someone, and ends up killing himself. We call an ambulance to take him away. Later I realize we don't even have a memorial service for him. I hardly know my son at all. He is a grown man.*

When I awoke, my son in the dream didn't seem like my son in reality. This made the dream a little less upsetting to me, though I wondered why I would have such a dark dream.

A few months later, events similar to those in the dream actually occurred. My son in the dream was actually a man I had been seriously involved with for a short time in Florida. When our romantic relationship ended, we remained friends. A friend from Florida called to tell me this man had committed suicide and had confessed in his suicide note to recently murdering two teenage girls. He also confessed to another murder years earlier. I had met this man at a church in Tallahassee where he was teaching *A Course In Miracles*. He had a very loving, very spiritual side. Everyone who had known him was in shock. The knowledge that I had been intimate with a man capable of such horrible acts upset me to the very core of my being. How could I ever open my heart to another man again? I fell into a deep depression.

Merlin later explained to me that I had always compared all the men in my life to my beloved father. I believed subconsciously that no one could be as wonderful as my father, that other men could not be trusted. These men in my life that obviously shouldn't have been trusted were an outward manifestation of this unconscious belief.

By loving my father so deeply, I had also given away my power. I had given it away to my dad, which was fine, but I hadn't as yet taken it back. Because I had given my power away to my father, it created a blind spot of sorts, so that I blindly trusted everyone and everything. Merlin assured me that when I brought my power back into myself, I would also bring the wisdom of how to protect myself, which is what my dad had done for me. It was time to grow up.

It was time to take into myself what my father had given me by not just keeping it out there in him, but by recognizing that he gave it to me. My father wanted to and did give me many special things. Now I had to receive them and be them and keep him inside of me through his gifts. This was accepting my own male energy. And the way to really honor my father was by taking into myself what he represented for me. Only when I was able to do that, would I be ready for the experience of being with another man in a strong and loving relationship.

*Chapter 22*

# The Quest

$A$s the winter snow melted into spring, I felt drawn to begin exploring the surrounding areas for my three special places of power. I really had no idea of exactly what I was looking for. The only things I knew for sure were that I would be guided and that I would know them in my heart when I did find them. But how far or near were they, and which direction? Were they on a mountain, in a valley, by a body of water, or simply a place in a meadow or the forest that called to me? I journeyed from my house wandering and wondering.

I had found a special place up on the hill behind my house where I liked to sit upon a rock and meditate. I could see in all directions — Mt. Shasta to the south, the town of Klamath Falls and Klamath Lake to the north, and surrounding hills, mountains, lakes, fields, and homes in all directions. Joining the many deer, rabbits, hawks, and eagles on the hill, I prayed, sang, and meditated as the sun disappeared behind the mountains. I felt at peace here and grew to love and appreciate the beauty around me. I wondered if my hill was one of my power places, but soon discovered that it was at the center of a triangle formed by my three sacred places.

I felt very much out of place and generally unwelcomed in my new community and close to only a couple of people. I continued to correspond with my German friend and fantasized that we may have a future together. I gave a few massages here and there, in my home or in my patient's. Once a week I began to visit a little town, Ashland, over the hills to the west for yoga, massage, good restaurants, and the theater. But in either place, my general feeling was one of loneliness in the physical world. My children were at that age where the last place they wanted to be was anywhere with their mother. So getting out into Mother Nature alone were my happiest times.

Through Joshua, one of my guides gave me a key to overcoming those times of loneliness and unhappiness. She said, "The way to overcome anything that is limiting is to be grateful for what you have. If you live in an environment wherein you are thankful, then you can be open to receiving much more."

So I concentrated on being thankful for this time spent with Mother Nature enjoying her beauty and her gifts and on beginning the great adventure of finding my personal places of power. I began to feel, however, that I needed more guidance as to where to look. So I consulted Lama Sing. I asked him to tell me about my lifetime as a medicine woman in the area and asked if he could help me find my power places. He answered as follows: "We are shown a triangular pattern which seems to be imposed over your geographical location with yourself being in the center of the triangle — an equidistant triangle — and if you were to draw a radii or a line to the upper left as you are facing approximately due north, you would find the corner of the triangle, so that the triangle is inverted, see, and on one edge. This seems to be the pattern of the three areas that might have the most impact for you. This covers, however, a goodly geographical area with the distance from your abode to the outward corner being fifty miles or so in North American measurement.

"And then from there, due east, see? In other words, heading to the northwest from your abode to find the outer corner, then due east would bring you to the other point at about fifty to seventy-five miles, approximate, and then also from that inner point, due south, you would find at approximately forty-five miles. Well, it's not an equal triangle, then. Nonetheless, at forty-five miles, approximate, you would find yourself in the foothills of some areas of particular spiritual heightening for you and others and particularly relevant to your past, as we see it here.

"The triangle, then, would seem to be the best approach for you to find those points, bearing in mind that it's not so much the specific geographical areas as it is the energy center, if you would think of it as such, that you are looking for; and as the mass mind thought changes and other factors change such centers, or anomalies as they are more appropriately called, do move a bit, but this is what we find. So to the diagonal, to your northwest, to the central point, then due south from there and due east from there (the central point) would give you the triangulation. See?

"It's suggested here that perhaps the eastward axis or line may not be as far as given. But what we'd suggest is to approximate this general direction of movement over the period for the next three to six earth months and to take your time in doing it — not looking for something with urgency, but with an understanding and open heart and mind, which can draw upon the forces of nature and those forces from the past to strengthen and to illuminate.

"It's important, too, to remember that as you receive guidance, to continue to question, to probe, to ask, to seek; for it's always important to remember that the highest and best information lies within self. Use this or any other such as might be given from outside of self, so to say, for perspective, for clarification by gaining more perspectives than just that one as might be found from within. But in the finality, decide from within. See?

"We don't have a specific town as such or even much of a location, for these seem to relate to a past life or lives wherein such factors were not permanent but transient. And, as such, also here we find the past relationship to these forces draws upon the native North American experience among a collection of tribes which were extremely peaceful and very industrious and very co-operative, highly ingenious in their methods of harvesting from the water and from the forest. They were unobtrusive residents in your area many, many hundreds of earth years before the present — your time. See?

"It appears here that your association as what could be called a keeper of the healing arts or medicines was by inheritance, in part, because of your family lineage and your association by way of those whom were your ancestors and then by the choosing or anointing of self through the ceremonies wherein such was confirmed. Your recognition as a practitioner of the healing arts which, in those times, seemed to strongly have to do with herbs, natural remedial forces as well as, of course, the spiritual works. And so there could be here an interest and perhaps some value in studying this lore.

"Certainly, some degree of faith is important here, if not required, but the greater asset in all of these things — all of these works and all of this searching — is to arrive at that state of joy within your being that knows no want, no doubt, no fear, accepts no limitation, implied or evident, and recognizes the eternal nature of self. Once you truly grasp and live in an attitude of eternity, you free yourself. When you look for, listen to, and live truth, you free yourself. When all that you do is preceded by an attitude of joy because of the understandings of the former, you free yourself. The peoples that you are thinking about and that you are searching for some link of heritage to, were above all else free and joyful. See? In the overall sense of your relocation, you have followed and indeed demonstrated, with good cheer, with good faith and hopefulness, guidance from within.

"And to the south and to the east and northwest. What is to be found here? Let these be joyous adventures. Share them where you can with your family, but always know that even when you might go forth on your own, you are never alone. The greater you can gain a sense of understanding and balance with all that is about you, the clearer will your path become. So for now, we do not recommend any formal establishment of a (massage) practice or a practitioner relationship, but as those are met whom are in need or interested or looking for some sort of support or encouragement, then give this. But in the interim, be in a state of ease and joy and explore, ask questions, and listen. Invite others to speak. Learn more about who is contributing to the mass mind thought and why. For remember that you live within the thought form of the environ as much as within the physical anomalies or structures which might therein be present. See?

"You have asked several times your purpose, your intent, what are you to do there. We would see this as a time of purging, a sort of re-orientation, a rebalancing, clearing out the old memories and habits. And as you do so, understanding what they have meant, bringing joy into the very essence of your life by freeing yourself from any limiting aspects of your past and thereby blessing all involved as you do.

"And now, looking forward and, as you have purified or released the past, look for a sense of utter freedom of spirit. Look for it in the land, in the waters, the forests, and all those things which are of such beauty around you at this time. This clearly is shown here as a time of cleansing, spiritual rebalancing — a sort of renewal, a sort of time for harvesting the experiences from the past and releasing those things that are no longer needed.

"This gives you, by the measure of the word here, immense opportunity, and while you might look upon this in some ways as being frustrating or boring or without the normal interchange or exchange between others of like mind, use your patience. See?

"Don't be hesitant to move out in greater and greater concentric circles from where you are in your explorations. You'll discover much, not only outwardly but inwardly as well. You'll identify, perhaps more clearly than ever before, what your true needs are — what Robin wants, what brings Robin joy. Then you can decide how to progress toward those goals. See?"

Lama Sing then addressed my question about whether, in a past life, I had lived very close to where I did now. His answer was that it was relative. He then went on to explain: "By your current standards, it could be considered very close. By the standards of those times, when no vehicles, as such, were present, it might have been considered a great distance. However, your peoples were somewhat nomadic, although they interacted with many of the other tribes to the north, particularly in (the) Washington state area, who were skilled fishermen and craftsmen and very knowledgeable. They were like a kindred group or tribe to you and your medicines, your knowledge — those of your people, that is, and including your own capacity in that area. Along with many of the things which you gathered and created from the environment, particularly the herbs and such, you brought to these people with whom you bartered and exchanged, not only fish but crafts and such. And so you often wintered with these people and traveled to the south of them, not very distant from where you are presently, and to the east and to the south and southwest a bit. See? Along the coastal area a bit more.

"The name, as we find it given, is given in translated terms and it, as best we can interpret it for you, we would understand to mean Shining Hand — obviously implying some power in the hand or hands that is to do with healing and healing works. Indeed, a name of some considerable honor. See?"

After being given such explicit and helpful information, I was anxious to continue my exploration. I visited the local forestry service office and bought detailed maps of all the surrounding areas relating to my quest and plotted out the areas that Lama Sing had specified. Exploring the land due east of my house, I spent some time at Dog Lake and Dog Mountain. A road led right to the top of the mountain, where there was a forestry service fire lookout. The snows had just recently melted, so the lookout wasn't in use yet. At least a two hour drive from my house, the mountain was about 7,000 feet high, and the 360-degree view was magnificent with mountain ranges, beautiful Dog Lake, and magnificent Mt. Shasta in sight. After visiting the area, I noticed I felt quite different energetically — lighter and more energized. I believed Dog Mountain might possibly be one of the power places I sought, but wasn't absolutely sure. I returned several times.

By the middle of May, the snow had finally melted in the area to the south of Midland in California. An hour or so away, this area seemed quite magical and was volcanic in nature, with cinder cones, "glass" mountains made of obsidian, lava beds, and beautiful forests.

In the third area specified by Lama Sing, or to the northwest of my house in Midland, the land and forests were beautiful, and there was a pretty lake that was an hour and a half or so from my house. I did not have any strong sense, however, of having found any of the three power places. I spotted deer, elk, antelope, and beautiful birds of all kinds during my explorations, and there were spring wildflowers everywhere! Wherever I went, however, the skin of Mother Earth was scarred with logging roads. No place was untouched by man's destruction, and I cried and prayed for the planet's pain and for her healing.

Chapter 23

# The Messenger

*J*une had arrived, and one evening as I climbed the hill behind my house to enjoy the sunset, a beautiful little hawk followed me all the way up, calling me with a distinct cry. The small, dark hawk flew swiftly and had a long, notched tail and long, pointed wings with a distinct white marking on the underside of each wing. I had never seen or heard such a bird. As I sat upon my rock, the bird circled me and then began doing aerial dives which ended quite close to me with a loud, vibrant buzzing noise. Startled, I wondered if I had disturbed its nest and was being attacked. Time and time again, it circled me, calling and diving.

# The Messenger

After a few minutes, I realized that there was nothing angry or menacing about my visitor, and I was able to let go of my fear. It was obvious that the bird wanted my attention. I mentally asked it what it wanted but received no response. As I walked back down the hill, it continued to follow and call to me.

Curious about the meaning of the visitation, I looked up the medicine of the hawk in the Medicine Cards book. I learned that the hawk is thought of as a messenger of the gods. While encouraging us to be observant of our surroundings, the hawk calls upon our intuition to know the meaning of its cry. The hawk's cry reminds us to be aware and open to receiving a message.

Each time that I hiked up the hill after that, about twice a week, the hawk would meet and follow me. And each time I asked what the message was but received no reply. Sometimes my feathered friend flew so close to me during its buzzing dives that I was afraid it would fly right into me! Other times, as I was inside the house thinking about making the climb, I would hear the hawk calling me.

Almost a month had passed since my first meeting with the hawk, and I was still puzzled and just a bit frustrated that I hadn't yet received or figured out the hawk's message. I had discovered in my field guide to birds that my visitor was a nighthawk. I felt a deep connection to the bird and looked forward to our meetings.

One day as I was hiking in search of my power place to the south in California, I had a strong feeling that I should hike up to the top of a crater I had passed by during other trips. As I followed a path which seemed to lead to the top, a bird flew from the ground near me, right across the path in front of me, and sat in a tree. As it flew, I saw that it had the exact markings that "my" hawk had. It sat in the tree not making a sound. I realized that the hawk had come to guide me to my places of power!

Thanking the hawk, I finished the climb to the top, where I discovered a magnificent view of the inside of the crater and the surrounding area. The trees in and around the crater were bent and twisted. The crater itself was quite beautiful, consisting of red, black, and beige rock. Tiny, fragile desert plants grew among the pebbles, and many were in bloom. A large hill blocked the view of Mt. Shasta, but in the distance I could see volcanic Mt. Lassen and in another direction, a beautiful little mountain of obsidian. My whole being was filled with joy for the discovery of this sacred place and its beauty, and I was grateful for the assistance of my spirit friends. I knew that one of them had taken the form of a night-hawk to assist me in this special way. I wondered if the bird would be present at each of the other two power places.

Just a week before discovering that sacred place, I had attended a workshop entitled "Sound Medicine" with Laeh Maggie Garfield, who is also the author of a book with the same title. On the morning of the summer solstice, Laeh told us that everyone has a healing song and that while she drummed, each of us would remember our song. As soon as we heard it, we were to go outside and sing it over and over again until it was committed to memory. Laeh began drumming, and in just a few seconds, it seemed, a very beautiful Native American-sounding song filled my head. Since it had only two words which were repeated over and over, it was relatively easy to remember. Everyone received a song, and we shared them with the group. One's healing song may be shared and even sung by others.

The next day Laeh told us that everyone also has a life or power song. This song is not to be shared with anyone other than the closest family members, or one's power could be lost or stolen. Once again almost immediately, my song came to me. It had many more words than my healing song and quite a different tune.

As I sat up on the crater that first time, I prayed, gave thanks, and sang my healing and power songs. I felt a deep connection to this place, the Creator, and the medicine woman deep within from another time.

Soon after this experience, I had two additional dreams about moving again. In the first, I had received guidance to move again and wasn't thrilled about it because I loved my house. In the next dream, we were moving because my younger daughter was part of a theater group in a different town, and it would be too much hassle to drive back and forth.

Meanwhile, my German friend and I continued to correspond. I had invited him to visit me, but he had not confirmed that he would. I dreamed that my ex-husband and I got remarried. Several of my dreams had indicated that marriage was in my future, and Mathias spoke often of the beautiful relationship that awaited me with this German man. I was still not certain, however, that this information was truly from Mathias.

The next time I hiked the hill behind my house, the hawk once again appeared. I thanked it again and was pleased that the visitations on the hill were continuing.

Just eleven days after the hawk appeared at the crater, I returned to Dog Mountain. Though it was the beginning of July and fire season had begun, I arrived at the top to find the lookout building empty. The sun was about to set, so I sat down to sing my songs and pray. Then as I began to sing a Huichol song, my bird appeared without a sound as it had at the crater, flew in a complete circle around me, and then flew away. I was elated to have another sacred place confirmed! As I drove down the mountain, the hawk flew across the road in front of me, and further down the road I glimpsed it again.

The search for my final place of power did not go as quickly or easily as the first two had. My daughters were in Florida with their father for the summer, and I felt lonely and frustrated that I had not completed my quest. Falling into a deep depression, I cried every day. Each time I left the house in search of my final spot, I realized that if I never returned, no one would miss me. My stomach was often upset.

I had scoured the area again and again, but had not felt particularly drawn to any place and had not seen my hawk. I felt like giving up. I was reminded of the time during my son's birth when I also wanted to give up. After two days of labor, I had been pushing for two and a half hours. I knew then, as I did now, that I couldn't give up, no matter how difficult it was.

# The Messenger

One day as I was hiking, I spotted a beautiful blue rock. Picking it up, I realized that I had seen a place nearby on a map called Blue Rock that I had not yet explored. My spirits lifted as I decided that finding the rock was surely a sign that my quest would end at Blue Rock.

The next day, on the first day of August, I drove to Blue Rock. It was actually the top of a mountain which overlooked a beautiful smaller mountain to the north that had a definite bluish hue to it. To the south, a peak known as Mt. McLoughlin rose majestically into the sky. It was evident that a fire lookout had once been atop the mountain where I stood, but all that remained were some stones that had served as a foundation. As at the sites of all the fire lookouts I had visited, there was a wonderful 360-degree view. Unfortunately, there was a family camping right at the top. Going past them, I found an isolated spot to meditate. My hawk did not appear. It was growing dark, so, frustrated, I drove back to Midland, crying all the way.

As I awoke the next day, which had been my father's birthday, I thought it would be perfect to complete my quest and celebrate his life on the same day. I decided to return to Blue Rock once again. As I turned onto the road which led to the top of the mountain, I saw the family that had been camping leaving. I hoped that meant I would be alone.

Alone at the top and seated on a rock, I had gorgeous views of both Blue Rock and Mt. McLoughlin, which were opposite each other. Singing and praying, I had a strong feeling that I should turn to look at Blue

Rock. Just as I turned, I saw seven golden eagles flying over the edge of the mountain towards me. Silently, they soared above me for perhaps five minutes and then left. Crying, I thanked them for coming. This must be my third place of power, I thought. I had finally completed my quest! I prayed and sang my joy.

But where was my nighthawk? Feeling confused, I left. Mentally asking my guides for clarification, I heard, "Expect the unexpected." I had to laugh at myself. Seven golden eagles — what a grand finale! I remembered that numbers have spiritual significance, and that seven is the number of beginnings and endings.

Chapter 24

# Magical Marriage

*Remember now many of the Master's teachings*
*about love. Love can set you free. Love is the*
*power that heals. Love is the power that surmounts*
*all and challenges nothing. Love exists as a*
*small particle or a great mountain within all.*
*You do not need a ritual, a rote, a dogma.*
*You need love. You need to live it, you need*
*to claim it, and you need to give it.*
*~ Lama Sing*

hree days later, I left for a gathering with Brant
at Mt. Rainier near Seattle, Washington. Mt.
Rainier is a very special mountain. A very strong feeling
of love emanates from that mountain. Brant calls it the
"dreaming mountain." One of my dreams was to come
true as a result of my being there.

I hoped that my German friend would once again
be present at this seminar, where I had first met him a
year earlier. I knew he had been on the East Coast ear-

lier in the summer. I was disappointed once again to discover he was not there, but probably my greatest disappointment was realizing I could no longer trust the automatic writing. It was obvious my own desires had tainted the information I had received from my guides. Merlin had encouraged me to begin to do the readings spoken, with a tape recorder. I hadn't felt quite ready for that. Now I saw no point to any of it. A friend later reminded me of how invaluable the messages from my guides had been, not only for myself but others, and she advised me not to "throw the baby out with the bath water." But I felt betrayed by myself, for I knew that I was responsible for the false information, and my heart was no longer in it. I sat down to do automatic writing for myself only twice after this trip to Mt. Rainier.

As I sat in the first circle of the seminar, I noticed a tall, gray-haired man with beautiful blue eyes looking for a place to sit. I invited him to sit next to me. It felt good being next to him. There was a very good, familiar energy about him. Over the next several days, we talked a lot. It was so easy and comfortable being around him. I learned that Scott was a Canadian and a surgeon. He was in the process of a divorce after 15 years of marriage. I started fantasizing about being hugged and kissed by him; it had been much too long since I had been touched by a man. Throughout the five days of the gathering, we spent much of our time together. Obviously, we had known each other at other times and in other places.

Several days into the seminar, I checked on things back in Midland. I was told that my house had been broken into and my car stolen and totaled. I was quite upset by this news, but Scott was there to comfort me. A deep attraction and passion grew between us. We talked about visiting each other, but I doubted I would ever see him again. As we said good-bye at the airport, he cried. I had seen very few men cry. On one hand, it was very endearing. Here was a man who was not afraid to express his emotions. Was our meeting so sweet that it had touched his heart so deeply? On the other hand, was he simply distraught by the divorce he was going through and "on the rebound"?

We spoke to each other on the phone every night, and as long as the conversations were, they never seemed long enough. We planned to spend Labor Day weekend together in Midland, but I was concerned that things were moving too quickly. I decided to let the drama unfold.

Scott told me during one of our phone conversations that his ex-wife was very upset about his new relationship with me and wanted him back. One morning, I awoke at 5 a.m. with a very strong feeling that someone was in the room with me. Looking around, there was no one physically there with me. But I could feel some very powerful and negative energy directed at me. I realized that it was a psychic visitation from Scott's ex-wife. She was very angry at me and held me responsible for his not wanting to resume their relationship. I began praying for protection, surrounding myself in light and asking that all energies which did not come in love and in the name of the Christ be gone. I felt the heavy, negative energy leave the room.

During this time, a close friend and her boyfriend came to visit me from Florida. We visited two of my places of power. As we were enjoying a beautiful sunset at Blue Rock, we were visited by a deer who ate the grass near us and allowed us to get quite close to it. Then an owl swooped down over us. I thought perhaps the deer and the owl were the guardians of this sacred spot.

I visited each of my places of power regularly. Each time, I experienced a sense of healing and balance and heightened energy. Sometimes my nighthawk would join me at Dog Mountain or the crater or behind my house on the hill. When I took another friend to Blue Rock one evening, the guardian deer visited, walking slowly in a complete circle around us before departing.

I received a sweet and loving card from my German friend. Even though there was a new man in my life, I still believed there was a possibility of a relationship with the German, or at least a visit from him.

A couple of days before Scott was to visit for Labor Day, I got cold feet. I didn't enjoy all the emotional turmoil I was feeling, and I was uncomfortable with the fact that he was in the middle of a stressful divorce. Relating my fears to him and also telling him about my attraction to the German, I told him that he shouldn't come. He said he was definitely coming — that it was too late to change his plans now. He called that conversation the "phone call from hell." I was an emotional mess — anxious, fearful, but also extremely excited.

We fell deeply in love during his visit, and I planned to fly to Canada in a month. I warned Scott, however, that I still cared for my German friend. Between visits we spoke for hours on the phone every night.

One night I dreamed that I went out to get some fast food. I was kept waiting a long time, so I left. Some employees ran after me, insisting that I pay. I yelled that I hadn't gotten anything there and didn't owe them anything. Then I was at a workshop where both my German friend and Scott were. The German was avoiding being close to me, and then he told me that he hadn't contacted me so that I could do and experience what I needed to. He then made me a fish dinner. Suddenly he turned into a fish and then inhaled some of the fish he had cooked and stopped breathing. Scott and I tried to resuscitate him, but he gasped and then died.

The dream made it clear to me that my fantasies about the German man had been temporary nourishment for me (fast food). I had waited for something to come of our attraction but had never received anything from my friend but nice letters and owed him nothing. The whole fantasy was like a "fish tale," something that I had "cooked up." It was time to allow it to die now that Scott was in my life.

Scott and I had only spent a total of ten days together but felt as though we had always known each other. Before my trip to Calgary to visit him, Scott asked me to marry him. Feeling pressured and extremely fearful, I told him I needed more time to make such an important decision.

We had a wonderful time during my visit to Canada. One evening we ate dinner at a Chinese restaurant in Banff. Discussing my fears and reticence to make such a hasty decision, we discussed what our plans might be if we were to be married. Telling him I felt the need for some sort of sign before I made a decision, we opened our fortune cookies. One of them said, "You can go ahead with your plans in confidence now." Ask, and ye shall receive. Having received the sign I had just asked for, I told him I would marry him.

Driving back to Calgary from the restaurant, I was unable to speak all the way home, I was so stricken with fear and doubts. What had I done, committing to marriage with a man I barely knew?

The next morning as we were lying in bed, I was thinking about my father, and I felt his presence. I thanked him for everything he had done for me and told him I had Scott in my life now. I saw Dad smiling down at us, and he said, "I am entrusting Scott with your care now."

Crying, I told Scott what had occurred. He, too, had felt his presence. It was such a gift to have my father's blessing. Remembering his words helped me to get through some very difficult times that lay ahead.

Later that day, we went to a New Age bookstore. There was a woman offering psychic readings there. As we sat down, the first thing she asked was if I was trying to get pregnant; she saw a baby. Then she added that she saw Scott moving. I had decided before meeting Scott that I did not want more children — three was enough! But falling in love with a man who wanted a child changed my mind quickly. Having finally released my fantasy about the German man, I had completely given my heart to Scott. We planned to get married during his next trip to Oregon in less than a month.

We were married in November of 1992 by a justice of the peace with both of my daughters present. We planned to hold a celebration with my son and other family and friends at a later date. Just after the ceremony, we climbed up on Mt. Shasta and prayed for our life together:

"This is our prayer, dear Father, that together as one we may serve Thee far better than if we were to stand alone, joining in the love that we share for ourselves, for each other, and for Thee in our common intent and purpose to live our lives as channels of blessings in the transformation of Mother Earth into truly an expression of Thy love and light. May we never place limitations upon ourselves or upon each other, but be of only the greatest support, encouragement, and enlightenment to ourselves, each other, and one and all. Amen."

The next months were tumultuous — Scott returned to Canada and applied for his visa while he gradually closed his medical practice and sold his home. It was six months before everything was in order for his move. In the meantime, we heavily contributed to the phone and airline companies. Before Scott moved to Midland in May, I suffered an early miscarriage. It was an extremely difficult time for both of us — Scott was so disappointed by the miscarriage as well as extremely stressed out by giving up his medical practice and moving from his beloved Canada; I was hormonally imbalanced and terribly upset by the loss of our child.

Through it all, however, I knew that ours was a marriage made in heaven. In truth, I believe that all of

our relationships are "made in heaven" by our agree-
ments made before we enter into the Earth plane. But
many of those relationships that are agreed upon to
contribute to our spiritual growth are not joyful. I knew
that this marriage was a very joyful gift to ourselves and
to each other. Mt. Rainier had worked its magic by
calling us. And we had answered.

Chapter 25

# Lama Sing Speaks of Love

"Love is the capacity of God within you to reach out and do a work. Love is a creative force that channels the River of Light to do a work or to simply be. Love is the association between the creator and the created. Love is a gift given from one friend to another through an action, word, or deed. Love is an essence that permeates your being, flowing from the center or your heart or your spirit, howsoever you wish to title it, outward from you when you are in balance. Love is blocked — as in terms of your capacity to receive same — when you are diseased or silent or bound by fear.

"Love is the essence that causes the plants to grow. Love is the fall of gentle raindrops upon a dry Earth. Love is that work which flows from your heart, mind, and hands when you set about to do a thing. Love is the embrace and caress of a child to its parents or a friend. Love is the gift of encouragement borne on the wings of one who wishes well for that person. Love is the essence that binds relationships throughout eternity. Love is the creative flow of the seasons, recognizing the need for all things to have their time and their harvest.

"Love is the essence of God borne as gifts within each of His children. And when given by His children, replenished ten-fold. You cannot give away love, because it is always yours. You can reach out with love and make contact with another entity or another thing. Once you have done that, you haven't given away a part of your love. You have connected yourself to them with what could be called a firmament of spiritual light. That firmament remains eternally. It cannot be destroyed. It can be ignored; it can be placed aside in terms of perception, but it is always there. That firmament of connective line of loving light between you and another entity can glow brightly with the unrestricted flow of your love to them and, in reciprocation, from them back to you. Or it can glow dimly when entities change their focus, their desires, and their goals. But it is always present, and the potential for incredible brilliance is always present.

"When you create a thing and you are joyful about what you are doing, a bond of love goes with that thing — whether it is a blueprint of someone's home or something that another will take your thought form and your energy of love and literally create in the Earth, or whether it is a few sentences expressing a regard for someone who is distant and reaffirming your caring for them, if not your love.

"If you dig a hole in the earth and plant a tree in it or a seed, you are connected to that seed ever more, and its fruits and their fruits and so on. When you disdain that thing as a labor, not joyful, the light is dim, yet present. See? When you connect yourself to a child because you love that child and you wish it to have the very best, that child carries the light of your love on as its heritage. And no matter whether the child grows to an adult and is aware of that or not, the presence of your light is within them and is a part of every good thing they do. Thus, you may return in a generation or two to harvest your own light. See?

"That is ascension. That is the cycle into which the Earth is moving. A time of love, a time of loving light. Those who will respond to this, whether great or small, can ascend. Those who will not, will need to do else than this elsewhere. Those who are liberated from the limitations and illusions can ascend, literally, as did the Master. Those who prefer to remain and to contribute can also do that.

"Love is the potential on which is borne truly the opportunity of every single dream you have ever held in your heart. There is no work that cannot be done by love. There is no obstacle that cannot be penetrated with an intent which is loving. You may not see the penetration in your time. You may not know that anything at all is accomplished. But that is God that you are giving, and there is not greater, is there, than God? And if you sow the signature of God's light lovingly in any direction to any individual, to any intent, that is an action which is eternal. See?

"When you identify love to another — a mate, a child who is born of your collective bodies — that is a love inspired by the creative spirit of God. God's spirit. See? It is created not only in the consummation of sexual relations and the biological, et cetera, et cetera, it is created well before you enter. There are joyful celebrations in that creative process, in the contemplations, in the review of the records, and on and on. When the child's body is literally before you, in part, to a considerable degree, the joy of that previous fellowship and brotherhood is one of the gifts that you feel, that inspires the recognition of your eternal nature and the gift that this opportunity provides you.

"But if you create a beautiful design or plant a seed that grows healthy and vibrant and bears fruit, learn to see those things in the same way. Granted, the one is another soul, another entity, who walks with you, dwells with you, and depends upon you, at least for a time. See these other actions in that same way, and you'll make remarkable discoveries that will serve you well. See?

"And note this: We have that on the Highest Authority. *Lovingly given*, of course. See?"

Chapter 26

## Upheaval

*I am looking at the largest, most beautiful tree on Earth. There are some children under the tree, and I am told we will learn from the children.*

In May of 1993, six months after we were married, Scott finally moved to Midland. My younger daughter was now the only child left at home. Scott was so excited about having a family and being a stepfather. That excitement was soon snuffed out as my daughter, who was almost thirteen, rejected this stranger in our house. And Scott reacted with shock and then anger at not being accepted into the family. Added to the stress of the move and beginning a new practice, this was too much! He also discovered that he related to my daughter in a very authoritarian way, which was not from his heart but his own upbringing.

The battle had begun, and I was in the middle. For a year the battle raged, with skirmishes here and there. The tension ran high, each considering the other the enemy. I did my best to keep the peace. The hormones were also raging — in the teenager as well as the couple deeply in love and attempting to have a baby. My daughter was experimenting with all those things most teenagers experiment with, especially when they're unhappy, and she developed an eating disorder to express her unhappiness and sense of powerlessness which she could not communicate verbally. The battle between my husband and my daughter would end with the birth of Scott's and my child.

Scott and I often visited my sacred places of power that first summer together. One night we camped out at the top of Blue Rock. We lay awake most of the night as many deer noisily surrounded our tent. Another evening as we watched the sunset from the crater, my nighthawk put on quite an aerial display for us, actually scaring Scott as it was diving very close to us time and time again.

As the summer drew to a close, we joined a gathering with Brant at Feathered Pipe Ranch in Montana where he performed a Huichol wedding ceremony for us. He also offered to help us, through shamanic prayer and healing, to conceive a child; but conception had not been a problem for us.

# Upheaval

The first time Scott and I had conceived, Scott heard a baby crying as we made love. About six months later, I had a sign that we had once again conceived — I saw a brilliant, beautiful flash of blue as we were making love. We were ecstatic when I missed my period two weeks later. Then I had the following dream: *I am with a woman, and we are ice skating through the sky. She is an expert, and I am doing quite well. I watch an airplane in the distance which will be pulling me on water skis. I realize I haven't skied in a long time, and it's a bit scary knowing I'll be up in the sky so high. I think I'll have to grab onto the rope very tightly. I ask what happens if I drop the rope, and I remember I'll have a parachute on which will keep me from crashing. I think there could be some danger landing, but I'll just have to deal with that at the time; I know how to bend my knees to prepare to land.*

This dream symbolized to me my fears of going through a pregnancy at 44 years of age. The danger of landing in the dream I interpreted as relating to the potential dangers of delivery.

Around this same time that we were experiencing all this turmoil and upheaval in our lives, Mother Earth expressed hers in the form of an earthquake. One Sunday while baking in the kitchen, I turned on the television. There was a movie on about an earthquake. The bread in the oven, I sat down to the last few minutes of the movie. At the conclusion, there was a warning with a long list of major cities in the U.S. at risk for major earthquake damage. Of course, Klamath Falls or Midland wasn't included, but I was still left with a feeling of disquiet.

I thought back to the big earthquake in California a couple of years earlier which had occurred while I was still living in Florida. I had awakened that morning wondering why I felt so energized, so physically different. Later in the day I learned there had just been an earthquake in California and knew that due to my receptivity, I had literally felt the energy of that event. For years I had been feeling energies from the Earth and from other people that most people had never felt.

That night in Midland I began to feel extremely agitated, negative, and angry. I didn't seem to be able to control my thoughts. The next morning these feelings intensified. The negativity I felt was overwhelming — I had never experienced anything like it before. Blaming my hormones, I struggled through the day.

That day I was also reading *Mary's Message To The World*, which is channeled information given by Mother Mary to Annie Kirkwood. Mary warns of the impending danger to everyone from the coming Earth changes and tells us what to do to prepare:

"The time is drawing near when you will be shaken and frightened, not because of any punishment, but to renew the lands and the minds of mankind. The Earth will shake and will be moved by violent forces which will cause many to lose their physical lives. The process which will cause these earth-changing events has already started. The changes have begun and will continue until completion....

"My desire is to warn you of the coming trying times. I wish for you to turn to God in your hearts and through your minds, for in this way some of you will survive these catastrophic events by renewing your spiritual values. Only in prayer and meditation will you find solace. Bring all your cares to the altar in your heart. Allow God to heal your hearts, your lives, your spirits, and your loved ones. This healing is your only hope, your only recourse. Only by prayer and meditation will you individually be led and guided....

"In the next few years you will see the hand of fate deal out some mighty blows to Earth. You will have earthquakes, volcanic eruptions, many large and damaging storms, and tidal waves of unheard-of proportions...."

In spite of a headache later that afternoon, I decided to go to Dog Mountain for sunset as I had planned. Scott and my daughter were busy elsewhere. I hoped to experience a healing there as I so often did. During the long drive there, the intense feelings of anger persisted. I sat on the mountaintop as the sun set, praying, singing, and meditating. As I began the drive home, I couldn't quiet my mind or the intense emotions I was feeling. A few minutes later I realized I had spaced out and missed my turn back to the highway. I felt disoriented and lost and realized I had gone several miles out of my way.

A few minutes later when I had returned to the highway, I realized that my anger and anxiety had totally dissipated. I felt as though a great weight had been lifted from my shoulders. I didn't understand what had caused such a complete shift on all levels. Only later did I learn that at home, about 50 miles away, they were experiencing an earthquake at that time.

Scott and my daughter were home when I returned,

and their eyes were wide with fear as they related their experiences. Soon I felt the intense emotions returning. Filled with rage, I yelled at my daughter about something. Suddenly, the house felt as if it were rolling, and then it shook violently as a strong aftershock occurred. My feelings of instability and intense emotion once again dissipated and were replaced by a feeling of numbness.

I had felt the energy of Mother Earth. I felt the pressure of the negativity upon the planet building deep within her womb. I felt the release, the cleansing, and finally the sense of peace the upheaval had allowed her.

We on our Earth Mother need to be aware that she is a living entity. As more of us realize this truth, as do the native peoples, and treat her with the love and respect she deserves, then the severity of the Earth changes can and will be lessened.

Chapter 27

# Initiation of a Different Kind

*Life, the Grand Illusion, for it seems so permanent
and so challenging, so much, often, all that is. Learn
that you are greater than this, and learn that love can
never be destroyed. It is like your own being, your
own spirit. It can only be transformed.*
*~ Lama Sing*

*A*bout five weeks into my pregnancy, I felt a gush
of blood. I had experienced a tear in the placenta and stayed off of my feet most of the time until I was
about seven months pregnant. At my own insistence, I
stayed behind by myself while Scott and the children
joined my family in Aspen for a week of skiing after
Christmas. It was one of the loneliest times of my life,
but it was an important time for my husband and family to grow closer. I gave up everything to enable the
pregnancy to continue.

Merlin told me that if I suffered another death along the way, it would be a death of my old self. We prayed for a healthy baby. It was a difficult time for us all.

I dreamed that a woman psychic told me that we would be making a sudden move. That same night, Scott dreamed that he was running through the slums of Montreal. He arrived at a train station. All of our stuff was there, and we had to decide what we were going to take with us.

We loved our home and the magnificent view of Mt. Shasta, but would not miss the communities of Midland and Klamath Falls when we moved. Spring had arrived, and I felt healthy and was having no more problems with the pregnancy.

We began checking into office space for Scott in the town of Ashland when we made our frequent trips over the mountain. Since I had first begun to visit Ashland soon after moving to Midland, I always felt as though I had come home as I came around the last mountain and was met by the beauty of the valley and the picturesque little town. We began negotiating to buy an office building very close to the hospital. Choosing a midwife in Ashland, we decided to have the baby there.

A couple of weeks before my due date, I began to go into labor, and Scott, my daughter, and I all drove to Ashland. As we left our house in the afternoon, I heard the nighthawk calling, reminding me that my friends in spirit were present. An ultrasound showed a healthy, big baby boy — perhaps nine or ten pounds. My older daughter joined us for the birth, driving a few hours from the town where she was going to college.

# Initiation of a Different Kind

Sitting in a birthing tub at my midwife's home, the warmth and buoyancy of the water helped to ease my discomfort during the contractions. After seven hours or so, the pain was unbearable as I stepped out of the tub to begin pushing. I wanted something for the excruciating pain, but we had planned on a drug-free birth, and there was nothing available. Squatting and pushing, I was supported by Scott on one side and my older daughter on the other.

A second midwife and my younger daughter were also in the room. As the baby was passing through the birth canal, my midwife began to have difficulty hearing the heartbeat. Both midwives began working desperately to help the baby out as the head crowned and the shoulders and tummy became stuck. It felt as though my whole insides were splitting apart. After a few minutes of pushing with all of my might and the midwives working to do everything they could do, our son was born.

Drained of every once of strength, I waited to hear the baby cry. I heard nothing. On my hands and knees, I was facing away from the midwives who were desperately administering mouth-to-mouth resuscitation and CPR. Someone called 911. At some point, I don't know exactly when, my midwife pleaded with me, "Look at your baby!"

The baby had looked at her and my husband and then closed his eyes, never taking a breath. I turned around and saw our son, still and lifeless. The cord was cut. I had no strength left to deliver the placenta. The baby was taken to the hospital in an ambulance.

Totally numb and going into shock, I realized that we would never hear our baby cry. I didn't care if I lived or died. I was sitting in a pool of blood, and the midwife couldn't get a blood pressure. Scott began yelling, insisting that I be taken to the hospital. After receiving fluids intravenously in the ambulance, I was able to deliver the afterbirth in the hospital. Part of me just wanted them to rip it out of me, as it felt my hopes and dreams and heart had been ripped from my body and my spirit with the death of my child.

Sobbing, we held our angel in our arms. Our baby was large — ten pounds and ten ounces, and there was nothing visibly wrong with him. I knew there was nothing or no one to blame, that for some reason he had chosen not to remain in this physical body with us. We had asked for a healthy baby. We had forgotten to ask, as well, that he live. Now he would only live in our hearts.

The horror had just begun. That night we stayed in a motel. The next morning my younger daughter was taken to the airport by her sister. She was to spend the summer in Florida with her father. She would have to grieve and process the emotions of the event thousands of miles away.

Twenty four hours after the birth, I was experiencing the most excruciating physical pain of my life. I was unable to move my legs or even sit up. The pain was unbelievable. My pubic bone had separated during the delivery, tearing tendons, ligaments, and muscles. The next day, as we were preparing to return to Midland, I was rushed again to the hospital shaking uncontrollably, chills racking my body as my temperature and blood pressure shot up.

I stabilized after spending some time in the emergency room, and then a friend helped Scott carry me to the car and then into the house as we returned to Midland. My hawk was there calling, welcoming me home.

Later that day as I was lying in bed, the phone rang. A young man I had never met was calling to tell me something about my older daughter. He said that because he cared about her, he wanted me to know that she was a drug addict, addicted to methamphetamine, or "crank." Hanging up the phone, I asked God how much I was expected to bear. He answered that we are given no more than what we are able to handle. I felt that someone had made a serious mistake here — that I certainly couldn't handle the pain of our son's death, being crippled, AND dealing with my daughter's problem. My dream had turned into a nightmare.

For over a week, I needed help to even have the bedpan placed under me. Crying together, Scott and I grieved for our son and also tried to deal with helping my daughter. Scott grew angry and impatient with my unending tears and the frustrating situation with my daughter. While I was crippled and thus unable to escape my grief, Scott buried the pain in his work and became numb to mine. He pushed me to sit up and begin to use a walker in spite of the intense pain. Setting simple goals for myself every day, I learned to stand with the walker, then take a step or two, sit in a chair, and finally make it to the bathroom with the walker after about two weeks. Then I learned to shower with the walker by myself, make it to the kitchen, then take a few steps without the walker, and finally to walk without bobbing like Charlie Chaplin. With the help of swimming and a dance class, I was walking normally in about three months.

Our son Teran's ashes sat on the windowsill. I knew he was with us in spirit, but my heart had been broken, and my womb had grown cold.

*Sudden deaths in the Earth happen so frequently —*
*not just in the loss of a loved one, a mate, a parent,*
*a child, a friend, a colleague. But the present is*
*destined to die, isn't it? Death in the sense that you*
*possess it only while it is unfolding. This is what*
*makes life in the Earth so extremely beautiful and so*
*filled with wondrous potential. The moment is a time*
*of creation which is ever present.*
*~ Lama Sing*

Chapter 28

# Teran in My Heart

*L*ife no longer seemed beautiful or wondrous to
me. Seeking a greater understanding and thus
acceptance of this dark time in our lives, I asked Lama
Sing for his perspective. It was clear to me that this experience shared with my daughters had resulted in a
deeper bond between Scott and his stepdaughters. And
Lama Sing assured me that not just the birthing process,
but the entire nine months of pregnancy had been an
experience which had strengthened me "in a manner
which perhaps could not be accomplished in any other
way to the measure and degree" as this process had accomplished for me.

We were told that Teran had not left and did enter the Earth, but did not retain the physical body because the choice at the soul level was completed. Lama Sing also told us about other lifetimes we had shared. In Atlantis, Teran had been a female who was a strong advocate of environmental healing and naturopathic methods. It was about 230,000 years prior to the Master's entry during the Atlantean period of enlightenment "where the retention of spiritual awareness transcended into the physical, to the point sufficient that many entities could easily attune themselves to what could be called the natural forces and could enlighten themselves spiritually regarding the history of any entity who was in a condition of dis-ease."

My function in that time was in that capacity of attunement, and Scott's was the application of various techniques and methodologies. Teran was a dear friend who supported our works.

The most recent relationship between Teran and Scott had taken place in Russia. Both were in male bodies and adventuresome, often challenging each other in sport. I was a member of the Russian aristocracy and very skilled in music, song, and dance. These pastimes brought me into their lands, and I was admired by both. While the differences were such that no permanent relationship was believed possible, both of them attempted to transcend that limitation. So there were many times of humor, of joy, and of cherished fellowship between us. And even though an ocean separated the three of us ideologically, our friendship never waned. This bond was perhaps the strongest and most familiar to bring us close together again in this incarnation.

Lama Sing explained: "The main purpose of the potential entry of Teran was not to renew this (bond) in the specific sense, but to focus upon the opportunity now present in the Earth for the forthcoming and present time of enlightenment. And that was the intent and remains so, that the entity might help two old friends — healers, each of you in your own right and in your own methodology — to contribute not only in terms of fellowship and support of your work, but remember this: that your thoughts were considered of utmost importance in the Atlantean times. And it is through these again that the entity will continue to walk with you both throughout the remainder of this lifetime and beyond, no doubt in service to the Master, the Christ — Amelius of old, the Christ of the present and throughout eternity.

"So sing a joyful song in your heart when next you think of this. For while you have lost in the sense of wonder, the joy, of a child entrusted to your care and guidance, you have gained a light upon your spirit, your soul, which is unequaled.

"Consider the event will be a memory within you, both of you, for an indeterminate amount of time as measured in the Earth. And it remains now that you have raw material, so to say, from which to build — to build upon that experience shared between you at such a level and intensity that cannot be expressed outwardly to one who was not present. And what shall come from this remarkable bonding between you? We can answer that for you, to a degree. Some of this is dependent upon choices to be made yet by each of you and together as comrades, colleagues, and such.

"There will be a reference point in your lives together from this point forward that will bring forth a new measurement of joy, a new focus upon the meaning of this day, this hour, this moment. You will look at one another and the events before you in life from a perspective which could not be ever considered by one who had not been through same quite to the degree that both of you will now have to your advantage. And while this may be a soft point of sorrow in the fabric of life, in the memory, in the experiences, there will be, perhaps, some degree of soreness, of sadness, of sensitivity for much time to come. And yet, we believe that you will immediately counter this with the strengthening each time it is thought of, of the bond between you.

"It is written here by entities of great light that the events of what might be seen in the Earth as times of deepest despair or sorrow are times when the spirit grows in brilliance to an immeasurable degree. Some would ask 'Why must it be so?' and the answer lies yet in the Earth, not here. For the manifesto of life and the events therein and surrounding such is yet being written by those souls who sojourn into the Earth and about it. And it is perhaps to this point that we would speak with the utmost of joyful encouragement to you both and to the entire family unit.

"Look for and take the joy offered to you in each day by a loving Father. And look to the events which are seemingly obstacles or frustrations or limitations with an eye which is opened and enlightened and which can see past and through these things as merely temporal, as merely those stepstones of opportunity, regardless of their judgment from the earthly perspective. The soul will ultimately rise higher and higher through each.

"So again, there has been exceptional growth and gain and that, of course, is understood, we believe, as you view this and hear these words. But we would tell you this: What lies ahead is the bounty from this harvest. Go forth and reap it with great joy and many thanks to the Father, for he (Teran) is with you, even as we speak."

Also according to Merlin, I had come through a very powerful initiation which had made me wiser and stronger. He told me that during the Crusades, I had watched my young child (Teran) being dismembered. I had tried to save my child but had been dismembered myself. During that lifetime, I did not understand that there is no death, only change. I had never forgiven myself for being unable to save my baby. It was time for me now, in this incarnation, to release the emotional memory of that lifetime and to accept that in that experience, as in the present, my baby had not truly died. Through the experience of his physical death in this lifetime, Teran was assisting me in receiving the knowledge that there is no death.

Merlin told me that Teran and I have been mother and child many times. I was once a queen on another planet. I had to leave Teran, my son, there to take charge when he was only twelve or thirteen years old because I was called to serve elsewhere. We promised each other then that we would always be together in spirit.

Merlin said that a long time ago, I had given Teran a part of my spirit during a time of great need for him, and that he had decided to return that gift to me during this lifetime. He was giving a part of himself to me to provide me with new strength, power, freedom, and light. With his gift, I would once again become whole. Merlin also reminded me that in the end, our experiences of joy equal our experiences of suffering. Our existence on Earth is one of duality where suffering is as important as not suffering.

I was told that Teran wants to be a part of our lives, and that writing him letters would keep this spirit, this consciousness, a part of our lives. As I wrote to my dear son, I expressed my desire to be more aware of his presence in a tangible way.

I wanted to touch him and to feel him. And not long after my letter to him, I realized he had found a way to touch me and allow me to feel him. I once again felt the familiar knocking at the door of my heart, insistent and frequent at first, until I realized that I was receiving an answer to my request. It had been a long time since my guides had let me know they were with me in this way.

The first two anniversaries of Teran's death were times of great emotional intensity for Scott and me. Not long before the first one, my back went out. Nothing helped. I was in so much pain that I was unable to do anything but lie in bed. I relived the physical and emotional pain of his death, then released it, knowing that Teran lives on.

A few days before the second anniversary of Teran's

brief visit with us, a deer and her fawn began hanging around the house, staying quite close. The fawn made a bed in the shrubbery close to the front door and remained there most of Teran's birthday. The next day they were gone.

We think of Teran often and feel his presence in our daily lives. He is never far. We receive his love and guidance, and his home on Earth is in our hearts.

Chapter 29

# Hawaiian Healing

*A*t the time of Teran's death, Scott and I were in the middle of negotiations to buy an office building in Ashland. Just two months later, we moved into the one-bedroom apartment above our new office. As in one of my dreams soon after moving to Midland, my younger daughter was interested in the theater, and Ashland would be a good place to develop that interest.

For six months, my two daughters and Scott and I lived in the apartment while we looked for a house. It was similar to experiencing a constant encounter group in those crowded conditions, which was probably helpful in keeping us from dwelling on the sorrow of our loss.

During that time, I had another early miscarriage. Lama Sing had warned me that if I ever got pregnant again, I would miscarry. Part of me had hoped he was wrong, which had never been the case in eighteen years of readings with him. The experience served to make it clear to both Scott and me that, after all we had been through, we were meant to put our energies into our work and each other and the three children who still at times needed our assistance and guidance. Our plates were full, so to speak.

After we had found a house and settled in, we went to a workshop on the island of Oahu in Hawaii with Diana, the woman who channels Merlin. Early one morning, we and the others in our group, about 10 of us, drove to the north shore. Dolphins regularly swim offshore there. A number of people were camped on the beach. They were there to drum to the dolphins, calling them towards shore, and to swim in the warm waters with them.

We put on our snorkels and fins and swam out toward the fins we saw breaking the surface of the ocean waters. The dolphins came and swam with us, playing and frolicking with each other and with us. Our hearts were touched and opened by the magic of their presence. Our time there in Hawaii was one of great healing for both Scott and me and helped us to rediscover the joy in our lives that had been missing for the past year since we had lost our son.

During that workshop, Merlin once again encour-

aged me to begin channeling through speaking and recording the messages rather than writing. He assured
me that I could channel his energy and guidance. Soon
after returning home, I began doing that and found the
readings done in this manner to be easier and more
convenient to do than the automatic writing had been.
Because of my past experience of receiving false information for myself, however, I decided never to do readings for myself again.

In the year since Teran's death, the magic had not
lived in my heart. But the workshop and doing readings
for others once again allowed the magic to reawaken in
my life.

Chapter 30

# The Owls

*L*ife went on, and the next summer a new challenge presented itself. My son had been going
through a very difficult time and came to stay with us
while he recovered. I was quite concerned about him
and did some healing work with him during his stay. In
the process, I managed to become imbalanced as well.
Needing healing myself, I drove to Blue Rock alone
one evening. I had continued to visit my places of power
at Blue Rock and the crater in California regularly since
moving to Ashland. Dog Mountain, four hours to the
east of Ashland, was just too long a trip since the move.

Depressed, I watched the sunset from my place of power that evening and thought about how my life hadn't had much magic in it lately — just a lot of chal-lenges. How I missed the magic! But then I reminded myself that the magic usually only happens when you are least expecting it. I began walking slowly, trying to forget my troubles and just enjoy the beauty of the pink sky and that special place. Suddenly, an owl swooped very close to me, just over my head, and then perched on the top of a tree next to me. My spirits lifting as a result of this unexpected visit, I thanked the owl.

Then, as I felt what I thought was the owl swooping close to my head again, I looked up at the tree to see it still sitting there. A second owl had appeared and then perched on a tree right next to the other! Tears began running down my face.

It was growing dark, and I thought that I should leave, but I really didn't want to leave while the owls were still there. Just as I had this thought, the two owls flew from the trees at the same time, very close to my head, and then disappeared. I knew they were saying good-bye. Remembering my very first visitation from spirit in the form of an owl near the top of Mt. Haleakala on Maui years before, I felt a special connection to the medicine of this creature.

Just before my son left to return home, we went to Blue Rock together one evening. I had prayed that, as a special blessing for him, the owls would appear. He needed some magic in his life. As we enjoyed the beauty of that place and the evening sky, the two owls swooped and circled us several times, and sat on their perches quite close to us in the silence of the night. I thanked them for answering my prayers.

Places of power were commented upon by Lama Sing during one of the Voyager Project readings as follows: "There are many things in the Earth that are in harmony with you, wherein a simpatico resonance can be found. Some entities find this in color, in certain stones or minerals, in certain patterns or designs or talismans. Certain types of plants, animals, seem to uplift or give strength to or enrich that individual. In the force of nature can be found the continual flow of God's power. Remember this: God's power is not stationary. It doesn't just go to a point and sit there. God's power is constantly in motion, and this is a very significant point that adepts learn very quickly.

"Those who are seeking to be one with the light and to be workers within the light will quickly realize that they cannot be stationary, static. Once they reach a certain achievement, once they reach a certain level of awareness or discovery, you can't just sort of nail your footwear to that level and plan to stay there for the remainder of that lifetime. Even though you might be able to do that in the figurative sense, the power is in motion. True, wherever you are, power flows to and through that place. But the greater wisdom is in finding where you are in greatest harmony with the power. For what purpose? To free yourself, to move with the power. If you go to a place of power, it isn't like going to a well and taking a cup of water from the well, and that's it. A place of power is like a radiant shaft of flowing energy. You can immerse yourself in this flow while there, and this, entity Robin, as you will remember, is why it has so uplifted you to visit these places of power.

"But back to the issue at hand. A place of power is a place of freedom, of strengthening, of replenishment, of harmony. It is that place that you find wherein your spirit can truly sing — where you can receive healing when healing is the need, where you can receive enlightenment when there is wisdom to be sought for a work, for a purpose, or where you can simply dwell and find profound peace, tranquillity, and joy.

"Now to the specifics of your question or questions, nature is bountiful. In fact, it could be said that all of nature offers to each entity all and greater than their need, no matter where they are. And yet, as the entity Robin has discovered, these places of power — anomalies, if you will — are like small confluences of certain energy flows that are just so in harmony and just so infilling for her that they are, indeed, truly places of power for her. Now, why can't she gain the same from any place, any locale? Perhaps the eternal truth of that is that she could. But as you all know in any finite realm of expression, eternal truth doesn't always seem quite as clear or as viable in some instances as it does in others — given with compassion and loving humor.

"The point is, if she stood in the midst of a busy intersection, would she not find the same power potentially present as she could at one of her other very special places of power? Certainly. The same energy is present there as in her personal power point or points. The difference is all those other thought forms, all those other energies, do not respect, do not even give acknowledgment to the presence of that power. In other words, it is severely veiled, diluted, et cetera.

"Now, certainly, Robin could attune herself to the primary power and tune out all the others. But would she be comfortable so doing? Would she require a greater expenditure of her effort to tune the other essences or energies out? And wouldn't it be easier, much more joyful for her, to find that place — the anomaly, the polarized points, you might call them — where she is in the greatest natural harmony with the forces of nature, the power of creative flow, that just being there is a joy? Of course, the latter is true. See?...

"The force of nature is loving and constantly seeking to nourish the Earth and all within and upon it. Therefore, no matter where you are, there is an anomaly within close proximity that would suit you. You will always hold some special reverence for past places of power and, indeed, you might wish periodically to make a special sojourn to those special places, simply because of that as a purpose or reason. But you will find that you will grow spiritually, just so as you move in the geographic sense in the Earth and otherwise, to seek out new places of power. Know that your growth is constant and, therefore, you might find an advantage to finding new, closer in terms of proximity, places of power.

"The force of nature, the creative force of life itself, anticipates growth and prepares for it. Thus, you have been prepared for where you are now residing. Seek those out in the spirit of adventurous joy, just as you did in the past. Remember?

And give it the same joyful dedication as you did

your previous places of power. See?

"Regarding the latter portion of your questions, it is difficult to summarize in a brief, general comment what these have given to you, and, conversely, what you have given in return to these places of power. For in order for you to have gained, you had to give, you had to seek. Remember, you put forth the effort, and this opened the way. And therefore, it could be stated in the broadest sense, in all things in the Earth, as you put forth that thought form, that intent, as you establish the ideal, purpose, and goal — all these things are enabling. They give permission; they grant authority within universal law. And they do much more than this. They empower you. And as you are empowered, then the true heritage that is always yours is awakened.

"As a daughter of God, you walk upon the Earth carrying His power with you. When you find a place of harmony and you seek it out with spiritual dedication — not that this shall be ever more a spiritual shrine, a place of holiness, for all of existence is holy, is it not? But to you, in that time, on this pathway, it is very special. And because you are empowered, it is empowered. And the next traveler upon a spiritual path who comes upon this special place will harvest fruits from your labor. And they, too, if they have wisdom, will sow their own seeds, that another will harvest like in kind. So what more transpired? You have given to the power of that place, just as you have received. For in your acknowledgment of it, this in and of itself is a blessing. Is it not?

"If you say unto a thing in the Earth, a living thing, 'I see you with eyes that behold beauty. I feel within my body the life that is good, the power that is pure. I feel within you all things that are good' — have you not, in those thoughts and words, those deeds, empowered that thing? So is it with your place of power. Never withhold the sense of joy and sharing to anything, any place, any individual, or any creature great or small, for in the giving of power do you receive it. Remember? God's power is always in motion. If you are the giver of His power, then the motion is from you to the recipient, and from God to you as the giver. See the power; know it. You cannot gain without the giving; for when the cup is full, it will only overflow. But if you direct its flow, then you become a part of that eternal flow and not a limited flow. See?

"So many lose their way here on this point. If you expect to gain a certain goal or achievement, a certain amount of wealth, a certain amount of this or that, and once attained you bring it unto yourself and you claim it as your own, and you hold it, you struggle to maintain it, you fight, you turmoil, endure turmoil, et cetera, et cetera, then what do you have? You have that achievement, and only it. But you, yourself, are in motion. Those around you are in motion. If you wish abundance in any aspect — be that spiritual, mental, joyful, be that in the material — the expression is irrelevant, see? The law is perfect.

"When Robin goes to a place of power, she gives. She gives herself, she opens herself, and she asks, 'How can I use what I gain from this place, this oneness? How can I use this in service to God?' And as she becomes sensitive to needs around her and she reaches out and fills those needs, then the place of power is ever with her, no matter where she is physically.... You cannot connect with the light of God and sever that connection by simply moving over here or traveling to this place or that. You must make the deliberate intent — or in some instances, not deliberate, unfortunately — but some action on your part must break that connection. See?

"Have an adventure. Ask nature: 'Where would you seek me to serve you and do you wish to serve me, this time?' Should everyone have a place of power? It wouldn't hurt. See?"

Not long after my son's and my encounter with the owls, Scott had a plastic surgery meeting in Dallas, Texas. In spite of looking forward to visiting my sister and her family who lived nearby, I was dreading spending time in the city. I always prefer being where I can more easily feel the spirit of Mother Nature. Cities usually feel so cold and spiritless to me, and I often feel disoriented and imbalanced in them.

Our first night in the city, Scott and I went to the top floor of our hotel after having dinner with my sister and relaxed in a hammock while looking at the night sky. Suddenly, I heard my nighthawk, and it appeared above us, circling. The message was clear — the magic can occur anywhere, anytime, and when we least expect it.

Chapter 31

# 1997: The Year of Healing Grace

*G*od has given me, and my children as well, the ability to heal others. He shows me what to do. I have a container of white liquid and a brush, and I am to seat the person I am working with, then paint him or her, beginning at the center of the person, or the solar plexus area, and move outwards in a spiral until the person is completely enveloped by the white liquid. This white "egg" should extend out past the physical body in all directions at least several feet.

I ask a man who is among several people at a gathering if he wants a healing, and he says yes. When he gets up with the help of crutches, I see that he is crippled. At the end of the treatment, he is able to walk.

*Some of the people present believe that the healing has not truly occurred but is a set-up, and that the man was never crippled. This doesn't bother me at all, because I know that he had been. I do some healings for other people, and as I do, I keep saying "God doeth the work; I serve as the channel."*

I awoke remembering this dream on December 6, 1996. A couple of weeks later, I received the transcript of a Lama Sing reading done for the Voyagers on that same date. Some of the Voyagers had called Al and asked to have some comments from Lama Sing about what the Master was going to be doing on Christmas Day. The following is from that reading: "He shall pass through the hearts of the infirmed and the dis-eased, those who stand before the veil of separateness, awaiting their movement or transition to the greater realms of glory which lie beyond. Therein, he shall instill a gift of hope and inspiration and insightfulness. These he shall give open-handedly so, as they will, they might partake of same. He shall in-visit each of those in the Earth who are incarnate and who are in service in His name. Those who are known and unknown shall equally receive from Him. He shall dispatch while so doing those who will be companions to journey through the forthcoming Earth year to those who have requested same. He shall impart simultaneously to those who serve others willingly, and to no intent of gain for themselves, greater blessings than we are capable of describing here.

"He shall, as ever, seek to awaken those who are willing and prepared to so receive such illumination. Especially, there shall be given in this joyful season the awareness of the power of God and His spirit as the light to guide same for the healing works. The forthcoming Earth year is annotated here as the year wherein the Christ gift of healing grace shall be at the forefront of all those good works.

"He shall, upon concluding all of these activities, seek out those who are in darkness and in pain in the Earth, and remain with them in the spiritual form throughout that day which bears His name. His joy, then, shall be to serve in this time of honor and celebration those who are, perhaps, the most distant from Him. And unto these, He shall give His greatest gift — His very presence. See?...

"The forthcoming Earth year, as we have stated, has been proclaimed here to be The Year of the Christ's Holy Grace, a year of healing. If ever you believed that healing in the name of the Master was or is possible, believe it during this forthcoming Earth year. This is a time wherein those things which are believed to be possible shall be done. According to the will of those who seek, it will be given. And you are afforded this rite of passage into Christ consciousness through the simple action of claiming it....

"So as we have given this commentary, we are cognizant that this may give the impression that this is a unique event or series of events. That is appropriate. And yet, this is always offered to those who will seek it. But in this instance, it is of a magnitude greater than has been present for some considerable Earth time. It is the beginning of the unfoldment and the preparation for those changes yet to come. It is the beginning of the illumination of the righteous and those who are upon said paths, that they might become known and that their works might be plentiful, abundant, and well-received.

"The question of doubt will oft come to the forefront. And when it does, cast it aside as easily as you would an empty container. For the only way it can have any meaning is if you fill that container with your own essence. Do not do this. See it for what it is, and cast it aside.

"When you find those who are in need or who are dis-eased and you align yourself with all that you know to do, and you offer all those prayers and works that are of your consciousness, then you have answered their need. You have fulfilled that which can be fulfilled. It is good for you to see that as the success of that work.

"Measure your accomplishment by what you feel, what you know, and by your own perception of your service to such entities as you and only you can adjudge. Fall not prey to the outward comparison that is continually attempted to be imposed upon you by the forces which are of the Earth. There can be no gradient of measure that is the equivalent of the sight that you will possess if you keep your faith, for that sight will enable you to see the greater healing work, which will be eternal. See this?

"You can heal as a channel of the Christ and see a dis-ease vanish. And you know that a good work has been done, even if only in the Earth. True? But if you claim the sight of the Christ, and you do that same work and the entity is healed in the Earth, and you also see the light about their spirit is ever so much more brilliant, then do you know that a goodly work has been done. And those who respond not at the physical, look to their spirit. Have you given light to same? Has the Master's light passed through you to illuminate that higher potential, insofar as ever they might be willing to release their limitation, that this light of His presence will in-fill and heal them instantly?"

After receiving the transcript of that reading, I was amazed by the congruity of my dream and that reading. Not only did they occur on the same day, both speaking of the potentials for healing on the Earth, but the dream even specified a method by which these healings may be accomplished!

Just a couple of weeks later, January 1, 1997, began with a flood in Ashland. Mother Earth was cleansing herself, washing away the old and reminding us that nothing ever remains the same. Her people here in our town, as they are all over the planet through natural disasters, were reminded that the truly important things in life reside within our hearts, not in the physical world around us.

At the same time that the flood waters were inundating my town, I was experiencing a personal cleansing — the worst case of the flu I could ever remember having. I recovered with a greater appreciation for my good health as well as the many other gifts and blessings in my life, and I looked forward to whatever the New Year would bring.

*We cannot always do great things in life,*
*but we can do small things with great love.*
*~ Buddha*

## Chapter 32

# Unification

*A*s spring arrived, I heard Merlin calling me. With the usual mixture of excitement for the new self-knowledge I would gain and dread of looking at those things in my life I have been blind to or hiding from my consciousness, I called Diana for a reading.

Merlin, the Magic Man, introduces me to the Great White Wizard of the North, who shape-shifts into the Great White Owl. I am told that I am being guided by him. Merlin encourages me to review my first book, *Messages From Mathias*, and instead of thinking of it as Mathias, to think of it as the Great White Wizard, as the White Owl. He tells me I was channeling a form of the White Owl. Merlin and he are brothers. And when I am channeling readings for others, I feel Merlin, but it is a different manifestation of Merlin. It is a very powerful channel that I am connected to.

I have always hated the cold. Merlin asks me what I think of when I think of the direction north. I tell him that *North to Alaska* comes to mind. Then he tells me of an actual lifetime I had there when my husband at that time met his death in a blizzard. Because he died before I had children, I experienced unfulfillment as well as abandonment.

I did, however, have very powerful connections with the spirit world and was often visited by the Great White Owl. I was often carried in my dreams to places of great beauty and wonder and safety. And it was from those experiences that I maintained and gathered my strength and weathered it through until the spring came and I would be reunited with my tribe and go on with my life. It was a very powerful and shamanic initiation.

I became an apprentice to that Great White Owl and one of the visionaries, or medicine people, of my tribe. Never remarrying, never having children, I nonetheless had a very powerful life. But this lifetime left the consciousness of a split between my physical and spiritual lives, and I was also left with my fear of the cold.

Merlin, in a guided meditation, has me go to myself during that lifetime as I sleep by the fire in my igloo. I appear to her as my future self and tell her that the experiences she has had in her dream time have been powerfully important to me and to my soul's growth. I have come to tell her that there is no separation. I tell her that I am in the future and that I am working with all of the blizzards in my life and in her life, but that I am determined to stay present, and that I am very warm inside. I thank her for being with me in this way. And she is also grateful to me because I have journeyed on to the next step, which is to make her realities of spirit a reality in the physical realm.

Merlin tells me that the next bit of work for me is all happening simultaneously as I pull spirit through my writing into the physical realm. As I begin to manifest this, I am making the union between my spiritual and physical realities. I am creating the absolute alignment with the moment. Many, many of my past lives will begin to appear to me as I begin to feel the pieces of unification coming in together.

According to Merlin, the Harmonic Convergence was the moment in which all of the lineages, mine and everyone else's, came into harmonic convergence. All of the different lineages that I and everyone else have experienced in all our different lifetimes became harmonious at that moment in time. As time moves on, the reality or the manifestation of that spiritual moment is beginning to occur inside of individuals. They are coming into the harmonic convergence themselves. As I gather myself and come into absolute physical awareness of the moment, I help create that essence of unity for all mankind.

The Madcap Magician from Mars tells me that the Hale-Bopp comet's light is the light of unity. As it moves through this solar system, it is sharing that light, and all the timepieces, or the great vortexes, around the planet are being activated. They have already been programmed

and are just waiting for that moment of activation, like the Harmonic Convergence was the moment of activation. The Hale-Bopp comet is carrying a light which will activate more unification.

The whole consciousness of separation and duality and living within these extremes of the paradigm is going to come to an end. This will take a good thousand years to actually manifest into the physical realm. But in my lifetime, this our lifetime, we will see many, many walls of separation coming down. The place where we will see it first is inside.

And as we integrate and unify more and more, we will see that this is also happening on the outward levels. Those places where we have felt empty and alone and abandoned and separate and cold will all be warmed. And we will begin to stand more and more in the middle and just observe the two extremes. More and more, our lives will come into a balance, a harmonic convergence.

Chapter 33

# The Magic Continues

*I* t is around the time of the Spring Equinox — a time of new beginnings in the Earth — and as I lie down in the evening to meditate, my puppy crawls under the covers to settle down next to the warmth of my body. We are alone in the house, and all is peaceful and still.

As I begin to speak to the Creator and to my guides, I feel the familiar activity in my heart, and at the same moment my puppy sticks her head out from under the covers and barks. The silence is otherwise unbroken, and I realize she has felt the presence of Teran. I am grateful

## The Magic Continues

for the validation, for even now, after many years of magic
in my life, I sometimes wonder if I am just dreaming;
and at the same time, I know that I am.

And the magic continues....

# Epilogue

*D*uring my last reading with Merlin, he advised me that an autobiography should not just be about this lifetime, but about many lifetimes and lineages, and the convergence of all that into now.

Relating my story has brought my spiritual life into the physical realm and has acted as a catalyst for unification in my life. It has made me remember a lot of the pain and struggle of my walk during this lifetime and others as well as the happiness. It has also reawakened a great sense of purpose in my present journey. It has once again filled my womb with the energy of creation.

# Epilogue

The honor and excitement of being a part of this time on Mother Earth are once again filling my heart with great joy. It is my prayer that hearing my story has renewed the hope and wonder and magic in your own walk at this time.

Each one of us that holds and acknowledges the light within has the power to change the darkness into light by allowing that light to touch each and every brother and sister, each and every creature great and small, the living Earth we walk upon, the precious air we breathe.

Listen to your dreams! Follow your dreams! Be open to the magic which lies in every moment if we are but open to it!

Know that you are never alone — that there are angels and spirit guides at all times surrounding you, enfolding you in their love!

Honor the Great Spirit, *your* great spirit! Honor all of life! Honor the most beautiful angel of all — YOU!

The magic lives within your heart.

Open up your heart.

Live the magic!